Paul's Letter Collection

Paul's Letter Collection

TRACING THE ORIGINS

David Trobisch

Foreword by Gerd Theissen

FORTRESS PRESS   MINNEAPOLIS

To Ingma

who made the words stand up straight

PAUL'S LETTER COLLECTION

Cover design: Patricia M. Boman
Interior design: Publishers' WorkGroup

Library of Congress Cataloging-in-Publication Data

Trobisch, David.
     Paul's letter collection : tracing the origins / David Trobisch :
foreword by Gerd Theissen.
          p. cm.
     Includes bibliographical references and indexes.
     ISBN 0-8006-2597-8 (alk. paper) :
     1. Bible. N.T. Epistles of Paul—Canon. 2. Bible. N. T.
Epistles of Paul—Criticism, interpretation, etc. I. Title.
BS2655.C36T 76 1994
227'.066—dc20   94–4746
                                                            CIP

The paper used in this publication meets the minimum requirements of American National Standard for Information Sciences—Permanence of Paper for Printed Library Materials, ANSI Z329.48-1984.   ∞™

Manufactured in the U.S.A.   AF 1–2597

98   97   96   95   94   1   2   3   4   5   6   7   8   9   10

Contents

Foreword

The Christian church has always read the New Testament as a literary unit. The Holy Spirit was considered to be the author of all of the New Testament writings. Historical-critical research, however, stressed that each writing be understood in its specific context. The New Testament was broken down by scholars into a number of separate books. At the present time historical studies seek to understand the New Testament once again as a unit. David Trobisch's book is an important step toward this goal.

Trobisch demonstrates that it is very likely that the oldest writings of the New Testament—the letters of Paul—already show a unifying tendency. His thesis is that Paul himself collected and edited some of his own letters. Using his correspondence with the Christians in Corinth, Paul composed two letters to the Corinthians, added his letters to the Romans and to the Galatians, and sent them all together with a cover note (Romans 16) to Ephesus. According to Paul's editorial concept, these four letters should form a unit and should be read together. The reason for producing this letter collection was the conflict with the Jerusalem authorities, who still considered the Christians as a Jewish group. Opposing them, Paul published this letter collection for his congregations, outlining what separates Christian views from the Jewish religion. At the same time, he emphasized that Jewish and Gentile Christians cannot be separated and, therefore, he promoted the collection of money for the Christians in Jerusalem in all four letters. With the publication of this letter collection Paul basically gave birth to the concept of a Christian canon—

that is, a collection of books that covers all the essentials that separate Christians from their Jewish mother religion.

You may not agree with every detail of this book, but the idea is fascinating. It offers a completely new picture of the origins of the New Testament. And, because the book is written in a clear, uncomplicated language, reading it is a pleasure.

Gerd Theissen
University of Heidelberg

Acknowledgments

A book like this, written in English by a native German, is the product of current research, friends, and colleagues both within and outside the field of New Testament exegesis.

Of critical importance was the contribution of Gerd Theissen of Heidelberg and Gerald Sheppard of Toronto for their valuable suggestions on style and substance. My thanks go to the faculty members of the Department of Religious Studies of Southwest Missouri State University in Springfield, who obviously enjoyed discussing central topics of my thesis and arranged for a lecture: James C. Moyer, Charles W. Hedrick, Robert Hodgson, and especially Wendell Willis.

I want to pay special tribute to Herbert Hanreich, Chang Kuen Park, Volker Gemmrich, and Markus Schwab, my Heidelberg helpers, and to Ingo Glückler in Aberdeen, Scotland, and Lisa Prince in Springfield, Missouri, who were gracious in their gifts of time at the various stages of the manuscript.

I want to thank my wife, Vera, and my mother, Ingrid, for their loving support of this project. In many ways it is their book.

The last word of acknowledgment goes to Marshall D. Johnson, Julie Odland, and other members of the editorial staff of Fortress Press who made this book eminently more readable than it otherwise might have been.

Note to the Reader

In the following work I invite you to join me on a journey back into history. I will introduce you to the oldest surviving hand-written editions of the letters of Paul. We will then visit ancient editors of letter collections and ask them to assist us in interpreting the work of their Christian colleagues when they put together the letters of Paul and formed the collection we now read in our New Testament. And, of course, we will spend some time with Paul, the apostle.

We will ask Paul what motivated him to write those letters and whether he expected that his letters would ever be published. We should be aware at this point that we are talking to a best-selling author. No other book of letters has ever been written, read, printed, and distributed so widely as the letters of Paul. And no other letter-edition in the history of humankind has ever sold and still sells as well as the biblical edition of the letters of Paul.

I do not expect you to know any Greek, although it will not hurt. Passages are quoted either from the New Revised Standard Version (NRSV) or from the New International Version (NIV). Only in very few cases I translate the text directly from the Greek to make my point clearer. You will find a note at these points.

For those who wish to study further, endnotes appear on pages 99–103. They are not necessary to read if you only join me on my journey, but if you feel like walking paths on your own they should provide you with useful information.

Let us get started.

1

The Oldest Extant Editions
of the Letters of Paul

Introduction

Before book printing was invented in the fifteenth century all books
had to be copied by hand. Approximately eight hundred early copies of the letters of Paul have survived to the current day. No two
copies are completely identical.

One of the reasons for the differences of text in the extant manuscripts is mistakes that occur when texts are copied by hand. But
there are other reasons as well.

Different Editions

Books have always been made to be sold. The text has been revised
over the centuries to meet the actual needs of the people who used
the books. Different needs require different editions. Bilingual editions for Latin-speaking students who were learning Greek were
produced; these provided the Latin translation between the lines or
on the page facing the Greek text paragraph by paragraph. Lection-
aries were produced to be read aloud by the priest during worship
services. Other editions added introductory passages to explain where
and why Paul wrote the specified letter. As with modern revisions of
the English Bible, old-fashioned expressions were changed to modern ones, and style was updated.

Some of the manuscripts are copies of an older copy. But often
the scribes would compare more than one older manuscript and
note all the differences in the copy they were producing. We do the
same today with our critical text editions: if there are differing

readings in extant manuscripts, modern editors decide which one they believe is closest to the original one and print it as the critical text, putting the variants in the apparatus at the bottom of the page (plate 1).

Most English translations do not give the reader all the information on the variants of the text. The same was true in ancient times. Only if the scribes were producing a copy for scholarly use would they carefully note variants and give explanatory notes in the margin. But if they were producing a copy for a broad audience, they would try to produce an authentic but understandable text, as free from scribal blunders as possible.

This situation applies to all ancient literature. The letters of Paul were passed on from one generation to another in essentially the same way as, for example, the writings of Aristotle.

Huge Number of Manuscripts

Compared to any other ancient Greek letter collection, however, the letters of Paul have survived in an enormous number of manuscripts

PLATE 1 (opposite)
Typical Page of the Greek New Testament[1]
The text of the page covers 1 Cor 2:14—3:3. The editors marked three words with superscript numbers 4, 5, and 1; these refer to footnotes. The footnotes describe different readings supported by text witnesses. For example, footnote 4 relates to the passage translated by the NRSV as (1 Cor 2:14): "Those who are unspiritual do not receive the gifts of God's Spirit. . . ." Instead of "God's Spirit" the old Ethiopian translation reads "Holy Spirit;" two Greek manuscripts (330, 451) omit "of God" completely. The omission is supported by several Christian and non-Christian writers when they refer to this passage, such as the influential heretic Marcion (second century); members of the Gnostic sect of Valentinians (second century), according to Irenaeus; one of the first known Christian interpreters of the New Testament, Clement of Alexandria (ca. 200 C.E.); his brilliant student Origen (died ca. 254); Jerome, who translated the Bible into Latin; and others.

The editors of the The Greek New Testament noted three variants they considered to be important. You will find a picture of the same passage from a bilingual manuscript referred to as manuscript "G" in the edition. I counted no less than fourteen minor differences not noted in the edition, nine alternative spellings, three synonyms used, one change of word order, and one additional word.

τὰ τοῦ πνεύματος τοῦ θεοῦ[4], μωρία γὰρ αὐτῷ ἐστιν,
καὶ οὐ δύναται γνῶναι, ὅτι πνευματικῶς ἀνακρίνεται·
15 ὁ δὲ πνευματικὸς ἀνακρίνει [τὰ] πάντα[5], αὐτὸς δὲ
ὑπ᾽ οὐδενὸς ἀνακρίνεται.
16 τίς γὰρ ἔγνω νοῦν κυρίου,
    ὃς συμβιβάσει αὐτόν;
ἡμεῖς δὲ νοῦν Χριστοῦ ἔχομεν.

Fellow Workmen for God

3 Κἀγώ, ἀδελφοί, οὐκ ἠδυνήθην λαλῆσαι ὑμῖν ὡς
πνευματικοῖς ἀλλ᾽ ὡς σαρκίνοις, ὡς νηπίοις ἐν Χριστῷ.
2 γάλα ὑμᾶς ἐπότισα, οὐ βρῶμα, οὔπω γὰρ ἐδύνασθε.[a]
ἀλλ᾽ οὐδὲ ἔτι νῦν δύνασθε,[a] 3 ἔτι γὰρ σαρκικοί ἐστε.
ὅπου γὰρ ἐν ὑμῖν ζῆλος καὶ ἔρις[1], οὐχὶ σαρκικοί ἐστε

---

[4] 14 {C} τοῦ θεοῦ p[11vid,46] ℵ A B C D G P Ψ 33 81 88 104 181 326 436
614 629 630 1241 1739 1877 1881 1962 1984 1985 2127 2492 2495 *Byz Lect*
it[ar,d,dem,e,f,g,m,r1,x,z] vg syr[h] cop[sa,bo,fay] arm Naassenes and Valentinians[acc.]
[to Hippolytus] Clement Origen[gr,lat] Eusebius Ambrosiaster Hilary Ambrose
Didymus Augustine ∥ ἁγίου eth ∥ omit 2 216* 255 330 440 451 823 1827 syr[p]
Valentinians[acc. to Irenaeus] Irenaeus[gr,lat] Clement Tertullian Origen Hilary
Athanasius Epiphanius Chrysostom Jerome Theodotus-Ancyra
[5] 15 {D} τὰ πάντα p[46] A C D* arm eth Valentinians Irenaeus[grms]
Clement Origen ∥ πάντα G Irenaeus[gr] Clement Origen Theodoret ∥ τὰ
πάντα or πάντα it[ar,d,dem,e,f,g,m,r1,x,z0] vg syr[p] cop[sams,bo,fay] Irenaeus[lat]
Origen[lat] ∥ μὲν πάντα ℵ[a] B D[b] Ψ 104 181 326 330 436 451 614 629 1241 1877
1881 1962 1984 1985 2492 2495 *Byz Lect* syr[h] cop[samss?] Macarius (Didymus
Theodoret πάντας) ∥ μὲν τὰ πάντα P 33 81 88 630 1739 2127 cop[samss?]
Chrysostom
[1] 3 {C} ἔρις p[11vid] ℵ (A ἔρεις) B C P Ψ 81 181* 630 1739 1877 1881 it[dem,]
[m,r1,x,z] vg cop[sa,bo,fay] arm eth Clement Origen (Eusebius ἔρεις) Cyril
Euthalius ∥ ἔρις διχοστασία 623 Chrysostom ∥ ἔρις καὶ διχοστασίαι
p[46] D (G ἔρεις) 33 88 104 181[mg] 326 330 436 451 614 629 1241 (1962 ἀρχοστασία)

[a a]2 a major, a minor: WH Bov Nes BF² RV ASV RSV NEB Zür Luth Jer Seg ∥ a minor,
a major: AV ∥ a major, a major: TR

---

14 μωρία...ἐστιν 1 Cor 1.23   15 ὁ δὲ...πάντα 1 Jn 2.20   16 τίς...συμβιβάσει αὐτόν
Is 40.13 (Ro 11.34)
3 1 Jn 16.12   2 γάλα...βρῶμα He 5.12–13; 1 Pe 2.2   3 ἐν ὑμῖν...ἔρις 1 Cor 1.10–11;
11.18

that provide a large number of variant readings; the result is that there probably is not a single verse of the letters of Paul that has the same wording in all surviving manuscripts. How should we deal with this discouraging situation?

Grouping Manuscripts

Fortunately, problems with complex manuscript evidence often are not as enigmatic as they seem at first sight. The trick is to find a way to reduce the enormous number to a small set of manuscripts to be considered. One way is to group manuscripts into families. This may reduce the number dramatically. For example, a paperback economy edition of the King James Version of the Bible looks a lot different from a deluxe study edition of that same King James Version. Yet, as far as the Bible text is concerned, both can be treated as printed copies of the same manuscript.

The majority of the extant manuscripts of the letters of Paul reproduce the Bible text as it was officially edited, revised, and published by the authorities of the Byzantine Church. I will call these editions the Authorized Byzantine Version.

The Authorized Byzantine Version

More than 85 percent of Greek manuscripts of the New Testament were produced in the eleventh century or later. At this time Christianity was no longer connected to the Greek language as closely as it had been in the second century when the New Testament came into being. From the third century on, the influence of the Roman church was steadily growing and with it the influence of the Latin translation. By the eleventh century the political situation of the Byzantine Empire had become more and more disastrous. Wars were fought and often lost against Islamic tribes in the South and against Bulgarians, Slavs, and Russians in the North. In 1054 the Byzantine and the Roman Catholic church separated. On May 29, 1453, the city of Byzantium was finally taken by the Turks, and the Byzantine Empire came to an abrupt end. For the Greek manuscript tradition of the Bible during these centuries this means that exemplars were produced, sold, bought, and used within a very limited geographical region controlled by the Byzantine church. Almost all manuscripts, therefore, reproduce the same Authorized Byzantine Version.

All manuscripts of the Authorized Byzantine Version can be dealt with as one single manuscript. The differences of text are the result of scribal blunders or the varying purposes for which the editions were produced and usually do not convey any knowledge of manuscripts independent of the Authorized Byzantine Version.

Fragmentary Manuscripts

Many manuscripts are not complete. Whole pages or parts of pages are missing. The vast majority of copies older than the sixth century actually provide only small portions of text, some of them being tiny scraps of papyrus containing but a few words. This results in the favorable situation that a large number of text witnesses are useful only for very small portions of the text. And because we shall look at the letters of Paul as a whole in what follows, the number of manuscripts to be considered shrinks further.

To be precise, by now we are talking about no more than eight manuscripts. Besides the Authorized Byzantine Version these eight manuscripts form the essential background for the reconstruction of the original text of the letters of Paul. In the next section I will introduce them to you.

The Manuscripts

Introduction

There is a good reason for dealing with manuscripts of the letters of Paul before dealing with the content of his writings—because these manuscripts are all that is left of the letters of Paul. We do not have any letter with Paul's handwriting on it. If, in studying Paul, one wishes to go as far back as possible, the manuscripts of his letters are the oldest extant form of his writings. Any knowledge older than that may be the result of learned reconstruction, but, like all reconstruction, it could be wrong. So it is important to start out at a safe point. The oldest editions of the letters of Paul are a safe starting point for our journey toward understanding Paul.

Notation of Manuscripts

Old manuscripts are usually referred to by the name of the library in which they are held or the library where they were first reported to be found. This applies to all old manuscripts, not only to those of the Bible. For example, a manuscript from the Vatican Library in Rome is referred to as a Codex Vaticanus.

The Vatican Library, however, treasures hundreds of New Testament manuscripts, so that a reference solely by the name of this library is not precise. Therefore scholars began to assign each manuscript, in addition to the library's name, a capital letter if the manuscript is written in majuscules, very similar to our capital letters, or a number if the manuscript is written in minuscules, very similar to our cursive handwriting. For example, the oldest known manuscript of the Christian Bible is called Codex Vaticanus (B). This system was introduced in the middle of the eighteenth century by the German scholar Johann Jakob Wettstein (1693–1754).

This traditional system, however, could not cope with the steadily growing number of majuscule manuscripts that were discovered in libraries and described for the first time during the following centuries. After the Latin alphabet was exhausted, scholars used Greek and Hebrew letters. But even the most sophisticated alphabet will run out of letters trying to classify the more than 270 majuscule manuscripts known today. Finally a third system was adopted: all the manuscripts were numbered. If the manuscript is written in majuscules, the numbers start out with a zero, for example *03*. If it is written in minuscules the manuscript is referred to with a simple number, for example *1739*. If the manuscript is written on papyrus, a "p" precedes the number, for example *p46*. Although this system of classification is very precise, most New Testament scholars find it easier to remember library names than numbers, and the traditional capital letters are still widely used. In what follows, manuscripts will be identified by all three designations, the name of the library, the traditional capital letter, and the numbers designed for scholarly use.

The Oldest Manuscripts of the Whole Bible

I shall now briefly describe the four oldest extant editions of the Christian Bible, comprising books of both the Old Testament and the New Testament. After all, the letters of Paul are only one part of the New Testament, and all the New Testament purports to be is the second part of the Christian Bible.

Codex Alexandrinus (A 02). The first manuscript I shall introduce is Codex Alexandrinus (A 02). It was written in the fifth century. Kyrillos Lukaris, Patriarch of Alexandria, gave it as a present to King Charles I of England in 1627–28. Today it is kept in the British Museum in London. This manuscript contains all the letters of Paul. Only a few pages are missing.

Codex Ephraemi Rescriptus (C 04). The Codex Ephraemi Rescriptus (C 04) also was produced during the fifth century. Originally it covered the entire Old Testament and the New Testament. In the twelfth century the ink was carefully washed off the parchment and someone copied the works of the Syrian church father Ephraem on many of its pages. The other pages are lost. If we look at the manuscript now, all we see are the writings of Ephraem. Ink, however, contains acid, which leaves marks on the parchment. With the help of modern technology, such as ultraviolet lighting, it is possible to make these marks visible and to read the original script. This *palimpsest*, the technical term for a rewritten manuscript, still provides 145 of the original 238 pages of the New Testament. Portions of texts from every book of the New Testament, with the exception of 2 John and 2 Thessalonians, are preserved. No book, however, is complete. The manuscript was brought to France by Catherine de Medici and is now kept at the Bibliothèque Nationale in Paris (plate 2).

Codex Sinaiticus (א 01). Codex Sinaiticus (א 01) is the only one of the four manuscripts still containing all the books of the New Testament. It was discovered in 1844 in the library of the monastery of St. Catherine at Mount Sinai and brought to Russia in 1869. In 1933 the Russian government sold it to the British Museum, where it is kept today as one of the great treasures of the museum. The manuscript probably was written in the fourth century.

Codex Vaticanus (B 03). Codex Vaticanus (B 03) was written in the fourth century. Nobody knows where it was produced, but it is recorded as belonging to the Vatican Library in Rome as far back as 1481. 1 Timothy, 2 Timothy, Titus, and Philemon are missing from the end of the manuscript. Each of these four manuscripts was written independently; that is to say, none of them is a copy of any of the others.

Number and Sequence of the Letters of Paul

While teaching seminars for theological students at the University of Heidelberg in Germany, I had an interesting experience. Very few of my students were able to tell me outright how many letters of Paul are contained in the New Testament. And out of a group of forty not a single student could give me the correct order of the letters. This

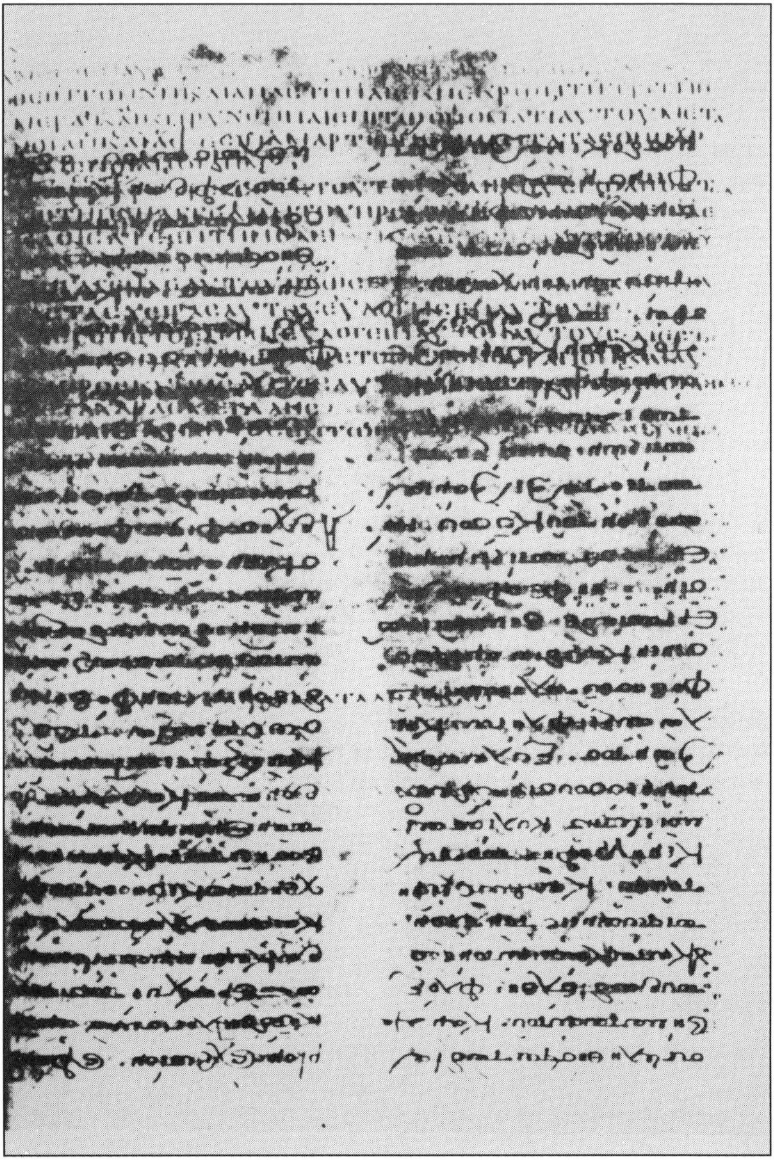

was all the more surprising in light of the fact that a high percentage of these students read the Bible daily and could recite by heart long passages from the letters of Paul, such as 1 Corinthians 13.

In the four oldest manuscripts described above the number of the letters of Paul is fourteen. Their sequence is uniform: Romans, 1 Corinthians, 2 Corinthians, Galatians, Ephesians, Philippians, Colossians, 1 Thessalonians, 2 Thessalonians, Hebrews, 1 Timothy, 2 Timothy, Titus, and Philemon.

The Four Literary Units of the New Testament

These simple observations teach us two important facts. First, there is an apparent difference between the four oldest editions of the New Testament and our modern English editions. In the oldest manuscripts, the letters of Paul are not placed between Acts and the general letters (James, 1 Peter, 2 Peter, 1 John, 2 John, 3 John, Jude).

Let me go into more detail. Many modern readers of the Bible have lost the feeling for the four literary units of the New Testament, and it is one of the goals of this book to get us back into touch with these units. Very few Greek manuscripts of the letters of Paul—to be precise, only fifty-nine out of 779—contain the whole New Testament. It was difficult to produce large books and very large books became heavy, awkward, and expensive. Most manuscripts, therefore, contain only part of the New Testament. The producers of manuscripts broke the New Testament down into four units. One of these literary units is the collection of the letters of Paul. Thus, we do not find an edition of a single letter of Paul in a manuscript.

PLATE 2 (opposite)
Codex Ephraemi Rescriptus (C 04)
All that appear on the original page are passages from the writings of the Syrian theologian Ephraem, written in cursive handwriting (minuscules) and arranged in two columns. To read this text one would have to turn the page upside down. For this reproduction the biblical text (end of the Gospel according to Luke) that was written first and washed off was made visible again with the help of modern technologies. It fills only one column and is written in capital letters (majuscules).[2]

When we read Paul's letter to the Romans, we read it as part of a collection.

TABLE 1
The Four Literary Units of the New Testament

Gospels	Acts and General Letters	Letters of Paul	Reve-lation
45.66%	19.57%	28.21%	6.56%

What are the four units demonstrated by the manuscript tradition? To put the Four Gospels in one unit and the letters of Paul in another unit is clear enough, but what about Acts? Surprisingly, Acts is always combined with the general letters. Some manuscripts begin with the letters of Paul followed by Acts and the general letters (Codices Vaticanus B 03 and Alexandrinus A 02), and some begin with the Gospels, followed by the letters of Paul, then Acts and the general letters (Codex Sinaiticus ℵ 01). Some manuscripts contain Acts and the general letters only. But with very rare exceptions no manuscripts exist that combine only the Gospels and Acts, or manuscripts of the general letters without Acts. Acts functions as the introduction to the general letters.

Actually, this combination makes good sense, for the main authors of the general letters—James, Peter and John—are the important leaders of the early church so vividly described in the first chapters of Acts. In later centuries the editors and revisors of the Authorized Byzantine Version started to move the letters of Paul between Acts and the general letters in editions containing the whole New Testament. The reason is not clear, but some scholars suggest that this arrangement was more convenient for use in church services. Whatever the reason might have been, it is clear from the older manuscript tradition that Acts and the general letters originally formed a unit. The Revelation of John forms the fourth literary unit.

The Letter to the Hebrews

The second thing we learn from the four oldest existing manuscripts of the New Testament is that the letter to the Hebrews is treated as a letter of Paul. It has its place directly in the middle of the collection, following 2 Thessalonians and preceding 1 Timothy. Although the exact place of Hebrews varies in later Greek manuscripts, this letter is always copied as one of the letters of Paul; it is not situated as one of the general letters.

The reason why my German students have such a hard time identifying the right number and sequence of the letters of Paul is that most of them grew up with the translation made by Martin Luther. Luther, like many learned Christians from the second century onward, did not think that Paul was the author of Hebrews. Translating the text, he rearranged the order of the New Testament letters, moving Hebrews, James, and Jude to the end, preceding Revelation. This does not represent the order of any extant Greek manuscript.

Most English translations and the bulk of Greek manuscripts from the eighth century on present Hebrews at the end of the letters of Paul, following Philemon. This was the normal sequence of the Authorized Byzantine Version. The first printed edition of the Greek New Testament was prepared by Erasmus of Rotterdam and published in 1516. He used only late Byzantine manuscripts of the twelfth and thirteenth centuries to produce the text. From this edition the sequence of the letters was passed on to most of the following printed editions; it remains the order of today's leading editions of the Greek New Testament (and consequently influences almost all translations of the New Testament). This order, however, does not represent the arrangement of the letters of Paul in the four oldest manuscripts of the Bible.

Manuscripts Containing Only the Letters of Paul

Not all of the manuscripts containing the letters of Paul present the whole New Testament. Actually fewer than 8 percent of all known manuscripts do. In most cases the letters of Paul were bound together with Acts and the general letters. And very often they were written in a separate copy containing no other New Testament writings as table 2 illustrates.[3]

TABLE 2
Number of Greek Manuscripts of the Letters of Paul
Arranged according to Their Contents

Contents	Number	Percent	
ap	271	34.79	
p	213	27.34	
eap	149	19.13	
apr	76	9.76	
eapr	59	7.57	
pr	6	0.77	
ep	5	0.64	
TOTAL	779		

e = Gospels
a = Acts + general letters
p = letters of Paul
r = Revelation

Apart from the four manuscripts mentioned, there are four others of equal importance for the reconstruction of the original form of the letters of Paul. All four manuscripts contain no New Testament writings other than the letters of Paul. Three of them are related to each other; the fourth is a papyrus book, the oldest known edition of the letters of Paul.

Codex Boernerianus (G 012). Codex Boernerianus (G 012) is a bilingual edition and very probably was produced in the monastery of St. Gallen, Switzerland, during the second half of the ninth century. The Latin translation of the Greek text was written between the lines by an Irish monk. It is kept today at the Sächsische Landesbibliothek in Dresden, Germany.

Codex Augiensis (F 010). Codex Augiensis (F 010) probably was written in the monastery of Reichenau, situated on the island of Reichenau in Lake Constance, Germany. Like Codex Boernerianus, it is a bilingual manuscript, but gives the Latin translation on the opposite page, corresponding line by line. It is now kept at Trinity College in Cambridge, UK.

In both manuscripts, five passages are missing in the Greek text. The scribes left some room to fill in the text later but never closed the blank space. Apparently some pages were missing in the manuscript from which they copied and no other Greek edition was available to them. Numerous differences between these two manuscripts can easily be explained by assuming that the exemplar they copied had notes added to the text, and that these notes were sometimes interpreted in a different way by the two scribes. Therefore, neither one is a copy of the other manuscript. They were produced independently, but from the same exemplar.

What makes Codex Boernerianus and Codex Augiensis so important? In both, the letter to the Hebrews is missing completely. The remaining thirteen letters are given in the usual order: Romans, 1 Corinthians, 2 Corinthians, Galatians, Ephesians, Philippians, Colossians, 1 Thessalonians, 2 Thessalonians, 1 Timothy, 2 Timothy, Titus, Philemon.

Codex Claromontanus (D 06). Codex Claromontanus (D 06), from the fifth or sixth century is somehow related to these two manuscripts. This too is a bilingual manuscript giving the Latin translation on the opposite page. Because of numerous distinct text-variants this manuscript shares uniquely with Codex Augiensis and Codex Boernerianus, their close relationship is evident.

The sequence of the letters is: Romans, 1 Corinthians, 2 Corinthians, Galatians, Ephesians, Colossians, Philippians, 1 Thessalonians, 2 Thessalonians, 1 Timothy, 2 Timothy, Titus, Philemon. No satisfactory explanation has yet been given for the unusual order of Colossians and Philippians. Originally three pages were left blank after Philemon, but later a Latin list of canonical books was copied there—the so-called Catalogus Claromontanus. Following this list the manuscript contains Hebrews. The evidence therefore suggests that Hebrews was not part of the manuscript that was copied to produce the Codex Claromontanus, but was added later.

Papyrus 46. The oldest manuscript of the letters of Paul usually is referred to as papyrus 46 (p46). Judging from the handwriting used in this manuscript, it is dated around the year 200 and was produced in Egypt. Parts of the manuscript were acquired by the University of Michigan in Ann Arbor, but most of its pages belong to the Chester Beatty collection in Dublin, Ireland.

This manuscript is not only the oldest extant edition of the letters of Paul but it is at the same time one of the oldest manuscripts in

> ο θε τοιс αγαπωсιη αυτον· ημιη δε απεκαλυψεη ο θс δια
τον πηс· αυτον· Το γαρ πηα· παντα ερευηα· και τα βαθη
τον θυ· Τιс γαρ οιδεη ανшн· τα· τον ανογ· ειμη το
πηα το εη αυτω· Ουτωс και τα εη· τω· θω· Ουδειс
εγηω ειμη το πηα τον θυ· Ημειс δε ου·το·πηα·τον
коσμου τουτου ελαβομεη Αλλα το πηα το· εκτου θυ·
ιηα ιδωμεη τα υπο τον θυ χαρισθεητα ημειη και λα
λονμεη· Ουκ εη διδακτοιс αηρшπειηнс· сοφειδс· λο
γοιс Αλλεη διδακτοιс πηс· Πηερματεικοιс πηερματει
κα· сνηκρριηομεη· Ψυχεικοс δε· αηос ου δεχε
ται· τα· τον πηс· τον θυ· Μωρια γαρ αυτω εстιη· και
ου δυηαται γηωηαι· Οτι πηερματικωс αηακριηεται
Ο δε πηερματεικοс· αηακριηει παντα· Αυτοс δε
υπο ουδεηос αηακριηεται· Τιс γαρ εγηω ηουη
κυ· Οс· сνηβιβαсει αυτοη· Ημειс δε ηουη κυ
εχομεη Καγш αδελφοι ουκ ηδυηηθηη λαλησαι
υμιη ωс πηερματεικοιс· Αλλωс сαρκεικοιс ωс
ηηπειοιс εη· χρω·· Γαλα υμαс· εποτειсα και
ου βρωμα· Ουπω γαρ εδυηαсθι Αλλ ουδε ετει
ηνη δυηαсθι Ετει γαρ εстαι сαρκιηοι Οπου γαρ

Teicht do roim mor rudo bec torbai INri chondaizi ri hi puss manimbera
Mor bair mor basle mor coll ceille mor Litr ni pos bai
mire ol air airchenn teicht do toinb beth fo toil· maic maire

book form known to exist. Up until the fourth century c.e. literature was copied almost exclusively on scrolls. There is some mystery about the origin of the codex (the Latin term for book in contrast to the scroll). Somehow the public use of the codex is closely connected to the formation of the New Testament. Christians were apparently the first to depart from the scroll and to use the book form as a medium.

This codex of the letters of Paul was made out of one single quire. That is to say, fifty-two papyrus leaves were put on top of each other and then folded in the middle, thus forming 104 leaves holding 208 pages of text.

If a codex is made out of one quire, the scribe must carefully calculate how much text the book will have to hold before he starts to write. Once he is past the middle page there is no way to correct a mistake, for any sheet of papyrus added at the end of the codex will give an empty first page. One can imagine how difficult the calculation was. Consider, for example, the problem of the inner leaves. When several sheets of paper were folded in the middle, the inner leaves would stick out and would be cut in order to make the book look nicer. This is what was done to p46 before the scribe

PLATE 3 (opposite)
Codex Boernerianus (G 012)
The text (1 Cor 2:14—3:3) matches exactly the passage given from the printed edition of The Greek New Testament above (p. 3). Capital letters structure the text and divide it into passages of comparable length, so-called *stichoi*. Many manuscripts still note the number of *stichoi* at the end of each book because the length was important to scribes, booksellers, and bookbuyers alike for calculating the price. The marks placed in the left margin indicate a quotation from the Old Testament and a Latin note identifies it as taken from the book of Isaiah. The Latin text follows the Greek word for word and is usually taken from the Vulgate, the most popular translation, but occasionally two alternative Latin renderings for the same Greek word are given. Because the scribe evidently had no other Greek manuscript available besides the one he copied, it could very well be that this bilingual manuscript was used for teaching Greek to Latin-speaking monks. At the bottom of the page the scribe, evidently an Irishman, added several lines of Irish, starting with the words "To come to Rome, to come to Rome, much of trouble, little of profit . . .," documenting the medieval rivalry between the Irish monks who were to be the first missionaries to central Europe and the authorities of the Catholic Church in Rome.[4]

started writing. This practice causes the inner pages to be smaller than the outer ones and therefore to hold less text.

For some reason, the scribe of p46 made a mistake when he calculated the amount of paper he needed. After he had filled more than half of the book, he realized there would not be enough room for all the text he planned to copy. He started to write more characters in each line and gradually increased the 26 lines per page in the first half of the codex to 28, then to 30, and in the end to 32 lines per page.

Although the manuscript is in fairly good condition, the outer pages did not survive. The text begins with Rom 5:17, then runs through Hebrews, 1 Corinthians, 2 Corinthians, Ephesians, Galatians, Philippians, Colossians, and ends in 1 Thess 5:28. Because many pages still provide their original page numbers one may deduce that the seven missing outer leaves holding 14 pages of text at the beginning left room for 14 corresponding pages at the end. The remainder of 1 Thessalonians, 2 Thessalonians, 1 Timothy, 2 Timothy, Titus, and Philemon cannot fit onto 14 pages of the size used by p46. A fair estimate lies somewhere close to 23 more pages necessary to hold all of the expected text. What the scribe decided to do, we do not know.

One should not assume that some of the missing letters were unknown to the scribe, although it is possible. The scribe evidently had difficulties with the length of the text. Two fragments of papyri codices contemporary with p46 have been found in the sands of Egypt, one of them, p32, preserving text from Titus, the other, p87, with text from Philemon, thus proving that these letters were known at the time and in the region where p46 was produced.

What caused the unusual sequence of letters? Why is Hebrews placed between Romans and 1 Corinthians and why does Ephesians precede Galatians?

The solution is very simple. It was crucial for a scribe to calculate properly the length of the text before he started to write a codex consisting of a single quire. In this situation he would arrange the different parts according to the length of the text before he started to copy the text. If he started out with the longest letters and ended with the shorter ones, the chances are good he could finish the codex with the end of a letter even if his calculation was wrong. In this case all the scribe would need to do is produce an extra volume out of some additional leaves holding the missing letters. If he were to start out with the short letters and end with the long ones, however, the chances are much higher that he would be in the middle of a letter when he reached the last page. And who would want to use a book that ends in the middle of the text?

So let us have a look at the length of the letters (table 3). Which is the longest, which the shortest?

TABLE 3
P46: Letters of Paul Arranged according to Their Length

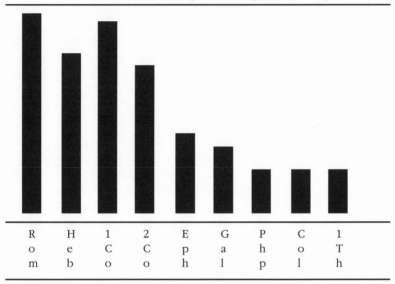

R o m	H e b	1 C o	2 C o	E p h	G a l	P h p	C o l	1 T h

Ephesians is longer than Galatians. Hebrews is shorter than 1 Corinthians but longer than 2 Corinthians. Nobody would want to separate the two letters to the Corinthians. An easy solution is to let Hebrews stand before 1 Corinthians. And that is exactly the sequence of letters in p46. So the producers of p46 arranged the letters of Paul strictly according to their length: Romans, Hebrews, 1 Corinthians, 2 Corinthians, Ephesians, Galatians, Philippians, Colossians, 1 Thessalonians.

The Archetype

Introduction

I was born in Africa. My parents were missionaries. My grandparents were missionaries. So it seemed very natural to me to view Paul as a kind of David Livingstone of antiquity.

I grew up with a picture of Paul traveling through Asia and Europe, founding congregations, counseling and teaching the men and women who had given their lives to Jesus. If he could not visit them, he sent letters. When Paul died, his letters were kept as treasures. Each church that had received one of his letters saved it, read it during worship services, and exchanged copies of the letter with other congregations close by. Later the congregations tried to complete their collection.

But this view does not match the uniformity of manuscript evidence. Let me explain. Today, before a book is published, the author presents a manuscript to the publisher. The publisher very often will suggest changes and will have the manuscript edited by professional editors. After author and publisher have agreed on the final version, a single manuscript is forwarded to the printer. This manuscript becomes the ancestor of the whole edition or, in other words, the archetype of the text tradition.

The view I grew up with does not suggest that there was any archetype of the letters of Paul. There were several collections and these collections were combined at different places by different editors until all known letters were included.

To determine whether a text tradition goes back to a single archetype, we must look for editorial changes that were made during the editing of the final version of the manuscript—changes not made by the author. For example if Paul did not collect and publish his letters himself, someone else must have added the titles of the letters and someone else must have arranged them. It is this final editorial touch that defines the archetype. The next step is to concentrate on elements of this final editing that are unusual and very probably would not be made by two independent editors. If all copies of the text show these peculiar editorial changes, they all derive from the same archetype.

Principle of Arrangement

How does an editor order the correspondence of another person? Nowadays editors try to arrange letters in chronological order when they prepare them for publication. And that is what editors tried in the days of Paul as well. But what does one do if the letters have no date?

Chronological Order? The letters of Paul are not dated. New Testament scholars have tried to assign dates, but a generally accepted chronological order of the fourteen letters has not yet been established. For example, one can argue that First Thessalonians was written during Paul's first missionary journey to Macedonia, thus making it the oldest recorded letter of Paul. Others date it during his last trip, making it one of his last letters, and their arguments are valid. In his letter to the Philippians (Phil 1:13) Paul clearly states that he is writing from prison. But scholars could not agree up to this day whether he was in prison in Ephesus, Caesarea, Rome, or some other place, and they consequently dated this letter very differently. The letters of Paul do not give enough information.

Nevertheless, two letters—1 Corinthians and Romans—give us almost certain clues to establish their relative chronological order.

> Now about the collection for God's people: Do what I told the Galatian churches to do. On the first day of every week, each one of you should set aside a sum of money in keeping with his income, saving it up, so that when I come no collections will have to be made. Then, when I arrive, I will give letters of introduction to the men you approve and send them with your gift to Jerusalem. If it seems advisable for me to go also, they will accompany me.   1 Cor 16:1-4 (NIV)

> Now, however, I am on my way to Jerusalem in the service of the saints there. For Macedonia and Achaia were pleased to make a contribution for the poor among the saints in Jerusalem.
> Rom 15:25-26 (NIV)

In 1 Corinthians Paul has not yet decided whether he will travel to Jerusalem or not. When Paul writes to the Romans his mind is made up. He plans to make the trip. By speaking of Achaia in Rom 15:26, Paul makes a clear reference to the addressees of 1–2 Corinthians because Corinth (1 Cor 1:2) is the capital city of the province called Achaia, and 2 Corinthians is explicitly addressed to "all the saints throughout Achaia" (2 Cor 1:1) as well.

Putting the information of these two passages together gives us the impression that Paul has just visited or is still visiting Corinth when he writes to the Romans. His fundraising campaign in Achaia seems completed, and he is determined to bring the gift to Jerusalem himself. This suggests that Romans was written after 1 Corinthians. However, Romans precedes 1 Corinthians in all manuscripts. Obviously the letters are not presented in chronological order.

Independent Arrangements. If the view I grew up with was right— that Christian congregations began with some letters and gradually tried to complete their collections of Paul's letters independently from each other—then each editor of the collection would have faced the problem of arranging the letters. It is very improbable that each one would have come up with exactly the same arrangement as it is given in the New Testament.

Uniform Sequences. The reason I think this would be very unlikely is that the principle behind the arrangement of the letters of Paul in the canonical edition is highly unusual. Let us have a look at the manuscripts again. The sequence of the letters is very much alike in the manuscripts I described above. Table 4 gives an overview.

TABLE 4
The Sequence of the Letters of Paul in the Manuscripts

1. Rom	1 Cor	2 Cor	Gal	Eph	Phil	Col	1 Thess	2 Thess	Heb	1 Tim	2 Tim	Titus	Phlm	
2. Rom	1 Cor	2 Cor	Gal	Eph	Phil	Col	1 Thess	2 Thess		1 Tim	2 Tim	Titus	Phlm	
3. Rom	1 Cor	2 Cor	Gal	Eph	Phil	Col	1 Thess	2 Thess		1 Tim	2 Tim	Titus	Phlm	Heb
4. Rom	1 Cor	2 Cor	Gal	Eph	Col	Phil	1 Thess	2 Thess		1 Tim	2 Tim	Titus	Phlm	Heb
5. Rom	Heb	1 Cor	2 Cor	Eph	Gal	Phil	Col	1 Thess						

1 = Sinaiticus (ℵ 01), Alexandrinus (A 02), Vaticanus (B 03), Ephraemi
    Rescriptus (C 04)
2 = Boernerianus (G 012), Augiensis (F 010)
3 = Authorized Byzantine Version
4 = Claromontanus (D 06)
5 = p46

In the first three sequences only the place of Hebrews differs. This can be explained easily by assuming that a collection without Hebrews existed and Hebrews was added to this collection independently at two different places. This process of adding Hebrews to a collection of thirteen letters is documented, as we have seen, by the Codex Claromontanus, where Hebrews is added later, following three pages originally left blank. This codex has the sequence Philippians and Colossians reversed. I consider this a minor variant.

In p46 the letters are arranged strictly according to the length of text as I demonstrated above.

Other Manuscripts. But what about the other manuscripts? Do they all have the same sequence for the letters of Paul?

I dedicated two years of my doctoral studies to finding an answer to this question. I checked all reports of unusual sequences that I could find, including existing manuscripts, reconstructed ancestors of extant manuscripts, old commentaries, citations by ancient Christian writers, the oldest translations, the lists of canonical writings issued by the Old Church and the very first references to the letters of Paul in Christian literature. As far as I know, this is the most comprehensive survey of this question ever made.[5]

In my research I could find only three more sequences (table 5). One of them has the same order as Codex Claromontanus, reversing the order of Colossians and Philippians. The manuscript, usually referred to as minuscule 5, is now kept at the Bibliothèque Nationale in Paris. It was written in the fourteenth century and contains the letters in the following order: Romans, 1 Corinthians, 2 Corinthians, Galatians, Ephesians, Colossians, Philippians, 1 Thessalonians, 2 Thessalonians, Hebrews, 1 Timothy, 2 Timothy, Titus, Philemon. On the top margin of the page where Ephesians ends and the text of Colossians begins, a comment was added that seems to have been written by the same hand as the manuscript, stating that the expected Philippians is to be found after Colossians. Thus the scribe was well aware of the unusual order and yet he did not change it. So the scribe probably reproduced the order of an older exemplar he copied.

TABLE 5
The Sequence of the Letters of Paul in the Manuscripts

6. Rom	1 Cor	2 Cor	Gal	Eph	Col	Phil	1 Thess	2 Thess	Heb	1 Tim	2 Tim	Titus	Phlm		
7. Rom	1 Cor	2 Cor	Gal	Heb	Eph	Phil	Col	1 Thess	2 Thess						
8. Rom	1 Cor	2 Cor	Gal	Eph	Phil	Col	1 Thess	2 Thess	Heb	1 Tim	2 Tim	Titus	Phlm	Heb	

6 = Minuscule 5
7 = Chapters in Vaticanus (B 03)
8 = Minuscule 794

The other sequence is preserved in the described Codex Vaticanus (B 03), where the text of the letters of Paul is divided into numbered chapters. These numbers do not fit the sequence of the letters as it is now presented in the manuscript. The numbers start with Romans and run consecutively through 1–2 Corinthians and Galatians. At the end of Galatians the number of the next expected chapter is 59 but Ephesians starts out with chapter 70 and goes on correctly through 2 Thessalonians. Hebrews follows 2 Thessalonians and starts out with chapter 59. This makes it obvious that in the manuscript where the division into chapters was made, Hebrews was to be found between Galatians and Ephesians.

The third sequence is even less significant. The manuscript referred to as minuscule 794 provides the letters of Paul in the usual order with Hebrews between 2 Thessalonians and 1 Timothy. A second scribe added Hebrews after Philemon so this manuscript today contains Hebrews twice. This probably happened by mistake.

Interpretation

I consider the reverse order of Philippians and Colossians in minuscule 5 and Codex Claromontanus to be a minor variant.

In all the other arrangements (except p46) only the place of Hebrews differs. And this, too, can easily be explained by the assumption that Hebrews was added later to a collection of thirteen letters of Paul. This thirteen-letter collection is still extant in Codex Boernerianus (G 012) and Codex Augiensis (F 010).

Two further observations confirm that Hebrews was added later: The uniform number of thirteen letters in the manuscripts and the titles of the letters.

Uniform Number of Letters. There is no manuscript evidence to prove that the letters of Paul ever existed in an edition containing only some of the thirteen letters. The last pages of a codex are very often lacking. The outer pages of every book are easily exposed to mutilation once the cover is lost. To conclude from the missing end of p46 or Codex Vaticanus (B 03) that some letters following 2 Thessalonians were not known to the scribes who produced these manuscripts seems unwise.

To retain the view of an independent grouping of the letters of Paul at different Christian congregations, one must assume that the collectors not only ordered the letters the same way but also had access to exactly the same number of letters—thirteen.

Uniform Titles. The other observation regards the titles of the letters. There is general agreement that Paul did not formulate the titles that appear in the New Testament when he first wrote the letters. One letter does not require a title. But a collection of several letters presented to a broader audience requires individual names for each letter. The function of these titles is to show where one letter ends and the next one starts, and to make it easier to refer to them.

All the manuscripts have the same titles for the letters. They name the addressee of the letter; a literal translation from the Greek is, "To Romans," "To Corinthians Number One," "To Corinthians Number Two," "To Galatians," "To Ephesians," and so forth.

This is especially noteworthy concerning the letter to the Ephesians. The three oldest manuscripts—p46, Codex Vaticanus (B 03), and Codex Sinaiticus (ℵ 01)—do not have an address in Eph 1:1, the only place where the Ephesian church is mentioned in this letter. But these manuscripts do provide the title "To the Ephesians." One does not have to be an expert to realize that scribes could easily have taken the address from the title and filled it in the text where they would expect it. This actually happened in Codex Vaticanus (B 03) and Codex Sinaiticus (ℵ 01); the later correction is still evident in these two manuscripts. But it is hard to think of a reasonable explanation why a scribe should have deleted the address from the text and left it in the title. Thus it is clear that the oldest text of Ephesians did not have an address in the text. How then could anyone figure out the title? No two independent editors would come up with the same name (plate 4).

PLATE 4
The Evidence in Codex Sinaiticus

A critical mark (~) is put between the lines. This mark is repeated in the margin indicating that the words EN EΦECW should be added here. The Ephesian address obviously was not part of the original text of the codex but was added by a corrector.[6]

Summary

To summarize thus far, first, the manuscript evidence can be interpreted to testify to an edition of thirteen letters of Paul with the order Romans, 1–2 Corinthians, Galatians, Ephesians, Philippians, Colossians, 1–2 Thessalonians, 1–2 Timothy, Titus, Philemon. Second, it is very unlikely that two editors would arrange the letters of Paul in this way independently of each other.

These two assumptions lead me to conclude that the canonical edition of the fourteen letters of Paul as it is presented in the New Testament today goes back to one single copy of thirteen letters of Paul, and that only the letter to the Hebrews was added at a later stage of the text tradition.

The Canonical Edition

Let us have a closer look at the canonical edition of the fourteen letters of Paul. The titles of the letters reveal two more interesting insights. They suggest an overall title of the edition, and they indicate the principle of arrangement of the edition.

Overall Title of the Edition

A collection of letters written by more than one author would naturally refer to individual letters by the author's name. But if all the letters of the collection are written by the same person, as the letters of Paul purport to be, there is no need to repeat the author's name in each title. Using the address to distinguish them from each other would be sufficient. On the other hand, a collection in which the letters are named by their address, like the letters of Paul, indicates that they all were written by the same author. The author's name becomes automatically the title of the whole collection. Therefore the titles "To Romans," "To Corinthians," and so on clearly suggest that the complete title is "Paul's Letter to Romans," or "Paul's First Letter to Corinthians," and that the overall title of the collection is, "Letters of Paul."

The oldest manuscripts, however, do not provide this overall title. Nevertheless, in many lists of the canonical writings and in most manuscripts of the Authorized Byzantine Version, this letter collection is called "The fourteen Letters of Paul." So the name of the book is "Letters of Paul," and the chapters received their titles from the names of the addressees of these letters.

Principle of Arrangement

The second insight the titles reveal is that the letters were arranged according to their addressees. Obviously, the letters with the same address are put together: the two letters to the Corinthians, the two letters to the Thessalonians, and the two letters to Timothy. Furthermore the nine letters that are addressed to congregations are grouped together, forming the first and longest part of the book ranging from Romans to 2 Thessalonians. This part is followed by the four letters which are, at least according to their titles, addressed to individuals: the two letters to Timothy, the letter to Titus, and the letter to Philemon.

Letter to Philemon. It is worth noting that the letter to Philemon actually is addressed "to Philemon our dear friend and fellow worker, to Apphia our sister, to Archippus our fellow soldier and to the church that meets in your home" (Phlm 1–2). As far as this address is concerned, it would be possible to arrange Philemon among the letters to congregations. On the other hand, since Paul writes to only one individual in the following text, it makes perfect sense to name the letter by the first person mentioned and to put it together with 1–2 Timothy, and Titus. There again a tight connection between title and sequence of letters is established.

Letter to the Hebrews. Before closing this chapter, let us look at the letter to the Hebrews again. The codices Sinaiticus (א 01), Alexandrinus (A 02), Vaticanus (B 03), and Ephraemi Rescriptus (C 04) place Hebrews after 2 Thessalonians. Because the letter is not addressed to an individual but to a group, "the Hebrews," it was added as the last of Paul's letters to congregations. The Authorized Byzantine Version places it at the end of the collection, following Philemon. The codices Boernerianus (G 012) and Augiensis (F 010) do not contain Hebrews at all. The different places in which Hebrews was inserted in the letters of Paul clearly indicate that at some time the collection consisted of only thirteen letters. Hebrews was lacking.

The title of Hebrews has the same wording in all extant manuscripts. This is especially noteworthy because the text itself does not suggest this title with a single word. It is very unlikely that any two editors independently from each other would have thought of this name. On the other hand, the title gives only the address; it does not give the name of the author of the letter. This implies that the reader knew the author. But how would he or she have known? Why did the reader of the canonical edition of the letters of Paul have good reason to assume that he or she was reading a letter of Paul?

To answer this question it is instructive to have a look at the general letters. A letter of Paul can be distinguished easily from any other New Testament letter. If we look at the New Testament as a whole, we see that the titles of the letters are designed to group them into two collections: The letters of Paul are named according to their addressees; the titles of the general letters give the name of their authors: James, Peter, John, and Jude.

As I have shown above, to name a letter by its addressee makes sense if the letter is part of a collection of letters written by one author. Therefore readers of the canonical edition will readily assume that they are reading a letter of Paul when they encounter the title "To Hebrews." The only place Hebrews is found in the extant manuscripts is among the letters of Paul. The uniformity of the title clearly demonstrates that all manuscripts of Hebrews go back to a single exemplar. In this exemplar Hebrews was already part of a collection of the letters of Paul.

Summary

We have gone back 1800 years to the oldest, handwritten editions of the letters of Paul. The oldest manuscripts we have investigated date from the end of the second century. Of the 779 manuscripts of the letters of Paul known today, not all are of the same importance. After grouping manuscripts and excluding witnesses with only small portions of text, only eight manuscripts and the Authorized Byzantine Version form the essential base for the reconstruction of the original text.

Looking at these editions we learned that the manuscripts split the New Testament into four parts: the Gospels, the letters of Paul, Acts and general letters, and Revelation. Furthermore, the uniform titles, sequence, and number of letters in the manuscripts indicate that the canonical edition of the letters of Paul derives from one single archetype. Although the letter to the Hebrews was added to the collection later, it is always part of the letters of Paul.

From the simple observation that the letters are named by their addressees, we learned that the overall title of the canonical edition is "Letters of Paul." The letters were arranged according to their addressees. The letters to congregations form one group (Romans, 1–2 Corinthians, Galatians, Ephesians, Philippians, Colossians, 1–2 Thessalonians, Hebrews); the letters to individuals form the second group of the collection (1–2 Timothy, Titus, Philemon). Letters with identical addressees are placed adjacent to each other (1–2 Corinthians, 1–2 Thessalonians, 1–2 Timothy).

Now that we have a picture of the text tradition of the letters of Paul, we shall investigate peculiarities of the text itself. We will make puzzling observations, encounter riddles that have not yet been solved, and discuss competing theories of interpretation that shed some light on the mysteries of the text. We will not be able to solve all the difficulties. It is the privilege of any ancient text to keep some of its secrets to itself, and it is a matter of honor to respect that. Nevertheless, it is an enjoyable part of our journey. Let us have a look at some of the characteristic features of the letters of Paul.

2

Characteristic Features
of the Letters of Paul

Inscription,
Expression of Thanks,
Wish of Grace

Most of the letters of Paul begin and end very much the same way. With the exception of the first paragraph of Hebrews, the inscription always consists of three parts: the name of the author of the letter, the congregation or the person to which the letter is addressed, and Paul's salutation. With the exception of Galatians, Hebrews, 1 Timothy, and Titus an expression of thanks to God follows the inscription. All letters of Paul end with a benediction of grace.

> [1] Paul, Silvanus and Timothy,
> [2] To the church of the Thessalonians in God the Father and the Lord Jesus Christ:
> [3] Grace to you and peace.
> [4] We always give thanks to God for all of you and mention you in our prayers. . . .   1 Thess 1:1-2 (NRSV)

> The grace of our Lord Jesus Christ be with you.
> 1 Thess 5:28 (NRSV)

Hundreds of ancient private letters have survived to this day. Almost all of the letters written in Greek begin with the name of the author and the address of the letter. Paul's salutation, "Grace and peace to you," however, is unique. Usually ancient Greek letter writers wish their correspondents joy, health, or simply greet them. Although passages expressing thanks to God following the inscription can be paralleled in a few cases, the uniformity in the letters of Paul is more than unusual.

Autographic Subscriptions

At the end of Galatians, 1 Corinthians, 2 Thessalonians, and Philemon, Paul remarks that he writes the last passages in his own hand. 2 Thessalonians states that Paul did that at the end of each of his letters (2 Thess 3:17). These passages usually are referred to as autographic subscriptions. They imply that Paul did not write the first part of the letters in his own hand.

> I, Paul, write this greeting in my own hand, which is the distinguishing mark in all my letters. This is how I write.   2 Thess 3:17 (NIV)

To dictate letters to a professional scribe was not unusual. The letters of Cicero are full of references to this practice. Scribes were trained to write in an internationally standardized script; they worked faster and made fewer mistakes than the average person, thus saving time and paper. In his letter to the Galatians, Paul acknowledges that he is not able to write as small as his scribe (Gal 6:11) and Paul's letter to the Romans even records the name of a scribe, Tertius (Rom 16:22).

> See what large letters I make when I am writing in my own hand!
> Gal 6:11 (NRSV)

> I, Tertius, the writer of this letter, greet you in the Lord.
> Rom 16:22 (NRSV)

On the other hand, it was not necessary to tell the addressee at which point the author would start the subscription. This would have been evident to the reader of the original. So it seems safe to assume that all the letters Paul wrote provided an autographic subscription, even those letters in which Paul did not explicitly indicate where the subscription begins (plate 5).

After having read hundreds of ancient letters, I would classify autographic subscriptions into three main categories. These categories may not be very sophisticated or complete but they fit most of the evidence. The reasons for adding a personal note at the end of a document have not changed very much over the centuries.

Authorizing Documents

The most important function of an autographic subscription—like a personal signature today—was to prove the authenticity of a document. It was not enough, however, simply to sign one's name; the author was required to write a whole passage. If he hired a professional scribe to write for him—and this was usually done for a legal

ΠΑΠΙCΚΩΙ ΚΟCΜ.ΤΕΥ
ΤΗCΠΟΛΕΩCΚΑΙCΤΡΕ
ΚΑΙΠΤΟΛΕΜ ΒΑCΙΛΙΚω
ΚΑΙΤΟΙCΓΡΑΦΟΥCΙΤΟΝΝΟ
ΠΑΡΑ ΑΡΜΙΥCΙΟCΤΟΥΠΕ
CΙΡΙΟCΤΟΥ ΠΕΤΟCΙΡΙΟC Λ
ΤΡΟCΔΙΔΥΜΗCΤΗCΔΙΟΠ
ΤΩΝΑΠΟΚΩΜΗC ΦΘΩ
ΤΗCΠΡΟCΑΠΗΛΙΩΤΗΝΤ
ΑΠΕΓΡΑΨΑΜΗΝ ΤΩΙΕΝ
ΤΩΤΙ IBL___ ΝΕΡΩΝΟ
ΚΛΑΥΔΙΟΥ ΚΑΙCΑΡΟC
CΕΒΑCΤΟΥΓΕΡΜΑΝΙΚΟΥ
ΑΥΤΟΚΡΑΤΟΡΟCΠΕΡΙΤΗ
ΑΥΤΗΝ ΦΘΩΧΙΝ ΑΠΟ
ΝΗCCΩΝΕΧΩΘΡΕΜΜΑΤΩ
ΑΡΝΑCΔΕΚΑΔΥΟ ΚΑΙΝ
ΑΠΟΓΡΑΦΟΜΑΙΤΟΥCΕΠ
ΓΟΝΟΤΑCΕΙCΤΗΝΕΝΕC
ΔΕΥΤΕΡΑΝΑΠΟΓΡ.ΗΝ
ΓΟΝΗCΤΩΝΑΥΤΩΝΘΡΕΜ
ΤΩΝΑΡΝΑCΕΠΤΑΓΙΝΟΚ
ΑΡΝΕCΕΠΤΑ ΚΑΙΟΜΝ
ΝΕΡΩΝΑΚΛΑΥΔΙΟΝΚΑΙCΑ
CΕΒΑCΤΟΝΓΕΡΜΑΝΙΚΟΝ
ΑΥΤΟΚΡΑΤΟΡΑΜΗΥΠΕCΤ

document—the document was valid only with an autographic subscription by the issuer. The author was expected to refer to one or two topics in the document as proof that he was aware of the contents of the document.

> A document (of divorce) in which there is an erasure or interlinear insertion in its body is invalid. But if it is not in its body, it is valid. If they repeat (the alteration) at the bottom, although (it has been made) in its body, it is valid.
>
> A document to which witnesses have subscribed after the salutation is invalid because they subscribed only to the salutation. If he repeats in it one item or two items from the context of the document, it is valid.
>
> Tos. Gittin 9:8-9, 334:6[7]

Autographic subscriptions are not restricted to legal documents; letters without autographic endings were apt to cause trouble as well.

Confidential Note

Next to the inevitable authorization of the letter, subscriptions to private letters sometimes have the character of a very confidential note. The secretary did not necessarily have to see the subscription, nor did he usually copy it for the archives. If the letter writer wanted

PLATE 5 (opposite)
Picture of P.Oxy 246. A Document with an Autographic Subscription.[8]
P.Oxy 246, Registration of Cattle. 66 C.E.

The sender, a certain Harmiusis, registers seven lambs. The return is addressed to Papiscus, an important officer, and to other scribes. The main statement reads: "I now register for the second registration a further progeny of seven lambs born from the same sheep, total seven lambs."

It is easy to see where the body of the text, a fine uncial hand, ends and where the cursively written subscription of the agent of Papiscus starts. The subscription reads: "I, Apollonius, the agent of the strategus Papiscus, have set my signature to seven lambs. The 12th year of Nero, the lord, Epeiph 30." (Epeiph is the month beginning June 25th.)

Following this—but not on the picture—are the subscriptions of two other agents, both repeating the date and the phrase "I have set my signature to seven lambs." It was essential for a subscription to a legal document to contain the name and some specification of the signing person, the date of the signature, and at least one topic from the body of the document (here, the seven lambs).

it so, no one was able to see the subscription until the addressee opened the letter.

Let me give you an example. Cicero wanted to share some confidential information with his friend Atticus. So after he dictated the letter, he started his autographic subscriptions with the explanation: "Now I write in my own hand. For what I have to say has to be treated with discretion." In this particular case Cicero did not even want his daughter to know.

> Now I write in my own hand. For what I have to say has to be treated with discretion. Please take care of the testament I wanted to make when she [Cicero's daughter, Tullia] started to ask questions . . . . Couldn't you advise her to entrust someone with her possessions, someone who is not affected by the dangers of this war. Maybe you? You would be my first choice, if she agrees.   Cicero, *AdAtt* 11:24:2

Addenda

Another kind of autographic subscription very common in private letters—my third category—is notes the letter writer for some reason did not dictate while his secretary was at hand. Often he simply forgot to do so. I fondly remember the letters my mother used to send me during my years in boarding school. Some of them she had neatly typed on her typewriter, filling the pages to the very last line. But the real treasures were all those small, handwritten notes she had forgotten to type, filling the margins to the last space. Often it was there where I would find such important information as who was going to pick me up, where and when. But let us look at an example from a family correspondence 2000 years earlier.

> I was just folding this letter when your messengers arrived today, the 20th, after travelling for 27 days. . . . (19) As I wrote these last lines with my own hand, your Cicero arrived and stayed with us for the meal, whereas Pomponia ate somewhere else. He gave me the letter he had just received from you to read. . . . I dictated the previous lines to Tiro while we had our meal together, so do not wonder why the passage is written by another hand!
>   Cicero, *AdQuintumFratrem* 3:1:17.19

Cicero had dictated a letter to his brother Quintus and had sent his secretary away when a messenger arrived and delivered another letter from his brother. Cicero answered immediately, adding notes with his own hand to the finished letter. He was still busy when Quintus's son, whose name was Cicero as well, arrived, and the two men decided to have a meal together. While eating, the nephew shares a letter he had just received from his father, and Cicero immediately orders his slave and secretary Tiro back to work. While the two Ciceros enjoy their meal, poor Tiro adds another passage to the letter.

Specific Information

It is characteristic for private correspondences to provide information that is of interest only to the addressee of the specific letter. This may be information pertinent only for a short period of time or it may be references to persons and events with whom the letter writer and the addressee are familiar and therefore do not need to describe more closely. Here is an example from a private letter written in the second century C.E. The original is still preserved and kept in the library of the University of Giessen, Germany.

> Heron to Heraclides his brother greeting.
> I beg you, my lord, to remember my request which I have made to you before your face. If on me you will not have mercy, nevertheless respect the girl and your daughter, and recall Saturnilus and his wife. [2nd hand:] I pray for your health, my lord.
> [Verso: Addressed] To Heraclides my brother.
>
> P.Giess.bibl.21.[9] (2nd cent. C.E.)

Who is "Saturnilus and his wife"? Why does Heron need to make a request? What had happened? Who wrote the wish of health—the girl? Who is "the girl and your daughter" of whom Heron writes to his "brother" and "lord"? The problem with private letters is that readers other than the original addressee usually miss much of the essential information obvious to the correspondents. Heraclides knew who Saturnilus was; he knew his relationship to Heron, he knew about the request Heron had made to him before his face; and he would recognize the handwriting of the final wish of health.

There is also the aspect of time, the right moment, so important for letter writing. Heron sent a note because Heraclides had to make some kind of decision. Once this decision was made, whether Heraclides complied with Heron's request or not, the letter had served its purpose. The correspondents could keep the letter or throw it away; it would not make much difference to them anymore.

I propose three categories of specific information characteristic for private correspondences: information pertinent only for a short period of time, proper names, and references to events with which the correspondents are familiar. Information suiting all three categories can be found in the letters of Paul. For example, information about travel plans or future visits of Paul is recorded in the last chapter of 1 Corinthians, and the very specific request to "bring the cloak" Paul forgot at Troas is recorded at the end of 2 Timothy. Once the addressee was informed, the purpose of these messages was fulfilled.

> After I go through Macedonia, I will come to you—for I will be going through Macedonia. Perhaps I will stay with you awhile, or even spend the winter, so that you can help me on my journey, wherever I go.   1 Cor 16:5-6 (NIV)

> When you come, bring the cloak that I left with Carpus at Troas, and my scrolls, especially the parchments.   2 Tim 4:13 (NIV)

Proper Names

The second category of information characteristic for private correspondences but difficult for later readers to interpret is references to living persons. Usually proper names will at least occur in addresses and final greetings of private letters.

> To Philemon our dear friend and co-worker, to Apphia our sister, to Archippus our fellow soldier, and to the church in your house. . . .
>   Phlm 1b-2 (NRSV)

> Greet Philologus, Julia, Nereus and his sister, and Olympas, and all the saints who are with them.   Rom 16:15 (NRSV)

Who are Apphia, Archippus, Philologus, Julia, Nereus, and Olympas?

Specific Events

The third kind of information is references to events that do not have to be explained in detail because letter writer and addressee know exactly what they are talking about. For example, about the only hint the letter to the Philippians offers as to where Paul wrote the letter is his mention of the palace guard and saints "who belong to Caesar's household."

> As a result, it has become clear throughout the whole palace guard and to everyone else that I am in chains for Christ.   Phil 1:13 (NIV)

> All the saints send you greetings, especially those who belong to Caesar's household.   Phil 4:22 (NIV)

Both references presuppose that the addressee knows where Paul is writing from and why he is "in chains for Christ." From our later perspective we cannot even tell with certainty whether Paul is talking about actual "chains" or whether the expression represents a broader reference to his suffering and imprisonment. It would make a difference to us if we had additional information on the events that led to Paul's imprisonment. Was he accused and convicted of some crime? Was he denounced, and if so by whom? Other Christians? Paul's own words suggest this possibility (Phil 1:15-18). But how can we tell from his sparse remarks? The addressees of Philippians evidently knew what Paul was talking about.

> The former preach Christ out of selfish ambition, not sincerely, supposing that they can stir up trouble for me while I am in chains.
>
> Phil 1:17 (NIV)

Passages with specific information are a common characteristic for any personal correspondence. At first sight, to find these passages in the letters of Paul presents no difficulty. The problem is that Galatians and 1–2 Thessalonians provide no such information at all. The final greetings of these letters and of 2 Corinthians are very general and give no specific names. This is not normal. Did someone deliberately cut out all personal references to names, places, travels, and all those trivial events that are so characteristic of private correspondences?

To look at this peculiar situation from a more general perspective, it is not the text we read that causes a problem, but the text we do not read. It is hard enough to find a suitable interpretation for an ancient text; how much more challenging it is to interpret an ancient passage that does not even exist! And this leads us to the next observation any reader of the letters of Paul easily can make—the letter collection evidently is not complete.

Missing Letters

First, Paul certainly wrote more than fourteen letters during his life. Second, the collection does not contain any letters written to Paul, although he evidently received letters (1 Cor 7:1: "Now for the matter you wrote about. . . ."). Third, the canonical edition explicitly refers to letters not included in this collection.

> *I have written you in my letter* not to associate with sexually immoral persons. . . .
>
> 1 Cor 5:9 (NRSV)

> For *I wrote you* out of great distress and anguish of heart and *with*

many tears, not to grieve you but to let you know the depth of my
love for you.   2 Cor 2:4 (NIV)

Even if *I caused you sorrow by my letter*, I do not regret it.
                                                           2 Cor 7:8 (NIV)

For some say, "*His letters* are weighty and forceful, but in person he is
unimpressive and his speaking amounts to nothing."
                                                          2 Cor 10:10 (NIV)

In his first letter to the Corinthians Paul seems to refer to an
earlier letter he had sent to them (1 Cor 5:9). In his second letter to
the Corinthians he twice mentions previous letters but his descriptions—"I wrote you . . . with many tears" (2 Cor 2:4) and "I caused
you sorrow by my letter" (2 Cor 7:8)—do not fit 1 Corinthians very
well. Later in 2 Corinthians (10:10) Paul cites Corinthian critics who
say "His letters are weighty and forceful . . . ," which indicates that
the Corinthians must have received more than one letter before Paul
wrote 2 Cor 10:10.

After this letter has been read to you, see that it is also read in the
church of the Laodiceans and that you in turn read the letter from
Laodicea.   Col 4:16 (NIV)

In light of the fact that the canonical edition does not contain any
letter to the Laodiceans, the letter to the Colossians seems to refer to
a missing letter.

Sudden Changes of Attitude

The next observation concerns 2 Corinthians only. In this letter Paul
changes his attitude toward the Corinthians without explanation.
Comparing passages from 2 Corinthians 7–9 with what Paul thinks
about the Corinthians in 2 Corinthians 10–13 reveals some glaring
contrasts.

I have great confidence in you; I take great pride in you. I am greatly
encouraged; in all our troubles my joy knows no bounds.
                                                           2 Cor 7:4 (NIV)

But just as you excel in everything—in faith, in speech, in knowledge,
in complete earnestness and in your love for us—see that you also
excel in this grace of giving.   2 Cor 8:7 (NIV)

But I am afraid that just as Eve was deceived by the serpent's cunning,

your minds may somehow be led astray from your sincere and pure
devotion to Christ. 2 Cor 11:3 (NIV)

For I am afraid that when I come I may not find you as I want you to
be, and you may not find me as you want me to be. I fear that there
may be quarreling, jealousy, outbursts of anger, factions, slander, gos-
sip, arrogance and disorder. 2 Cor 12:20 (NIV)

First Paul speaks highly of the Corinthians, and then he reproaches
them. In 2 Corinthians 10–13 Paul does not find a positive word
to describe the Corinthians. No reason is given why he so dramatically changes his mind. If he had received bad news while writing
2 Corinthians, why did he not delete the flattering passages he had
already written from the letter he was going to send? This change of
attitude cannot be paralleled in any of the other letters of Paul.[10]

The problem of the changed attitude of Paul toward the Corinthians in 2 Corinthians was the first exegetical problem that really
fascinated me. I read all the interpretations and explanations I could
find, but the answers did not satisfy me. The more I read the more I
realized that there is no widely accepted interpretation of this situation today. There are several brilliant conjectures that try to explain
the phenomenon by assuming that the original Pauline text was
rearranged and distorted by later editors. But no one could tell me
what the final editors had in mind when they produced 2 Corinthians. What I was looking for was an explanation that would help
me understand the text of 2 Corinthians as we read it in the canonical edition. To find a solution became a hobby of mine. I started to
look at similar ancient letter collections. Gradually I developed a
theory which I will relate in the next chapter.

Unexpected Digressions

The next observation I want to make is just as mysterious. There are
a number of passages in the letters of Paul that if deleted from the
text would make the text read more smoothly. I call those passages
"unexpected digressions." They treat topics that are only loosely
related to the context, and thus, they appear to be passages that
were added at a later time.

For example, if we delete 1 Cor 12:31b—14:1a, more than a
whole chapter, the text reads (NRSV):

Now you are the body of Christ and individually members of it. And

God has appointed in the church first apostles, second prophets, third teachers; then deeds of power, then gifts of healing, forms of assistance, forms of leadership, various kinds of tongues.

Are all apostles? Are all prophets? Are all teachers? Do all work miracles? Do all possess gifts of healing? Do all speak in tongues? Do all interpret?

But strive for the greater gifts, and especially that you may prophesy. For those who speak in a tongue do not speak to other people but to God; for nobody understands them, since they are speaking mysteries in the Spirit. On the other hand, those who prophesy speak to other people for their upbuilding and encouragement and consolation.

To identify the point in the above passage at which a whole chapter was deleted is a difficult task. Paul is talking about speaking in tongues and the gift of prophecy. Actually, without the digression the text suggests that the most desirable gift is the gift of prophecy. The theme of the digression, however, is love.

The introduction and the end of 1 Corinthians 13 (NRSV) read as follows:

[But strive for the greater gifts]. And I will show you a still more excellent way. If I speak in the tongues of mortals and of angels, but do not have love, I am a noisy gong or a clanging cymbal. . . . And now faith, hope and love abide, these three; and the greatest of these is love. Pursue love and strive for the spiritual gifts[, and especially that you may prophesy].

1 Corinthians 13 makes a connection to the topic of prophecy and speaking in tongues treated in the immediate context, by choosing speaking in tongues as the first example presented in 1 Corinthians 13. Then there is a connection between the expression "strive for the greater gifts" and "the greatest of these is love." The passage ends by repeating almost exactly the same words it began with: "Strive for the spiritual gifts." The context does not require this digression at all; actually the word *love* is not even used in the text of 1 Corinthians 12. Although there is no immediate need to assume that 1 Corinthians 13 was added later, it remains a possible explanation. By repeating the preceding text at the end of the passage, 1 Corinthians 13 still tells the reader how it is connected to the surrounding text. There are other digressions, however, where the connection is difficult to understand.

A well-known passage is found in the following chapter, 1 Cor

14:34-35. Paul is still dealing with the topic of prophecy. I will give you the surrounding text without this passage (NIV):

> And if a revelation comes to someone who is sitting down, the first speaker should stop. For you can all prophesy in turn so that everyone may be instructed and encouraged. The spirits of prophets are subject to the control of prophets. For God is not a God of disorder but of peace as all the congregations of the saints believe. Did the word of God originate with you? Or are you the only people it has reached? If anybody thinks he is a prophet or spiritually gifted, let him acknowledge that what I am writing to you is the Lord's command. If he ignores this, he himself will be ignored.[11]

Paul wants the prophets not to talk all at the same time but to take turns. They should be able to do so, because Christian prophets are in control of their spirits. This is what Jesus said and what all the other Christian congregations believe. So if prophets cannot control their spirits, the congregation should not pay any further attention to them, but simply ignore them.

The passage 1 Cor 14:34-35 (NIV) changes abruptly to another subject:

> [For God is not a God of disorder but of peace. As in all the congregations of the saints,] women should remain silent in the churches. They are not allowed to speak, but must be in submission, as the Law says. If they want to inquire about something, they should ask their own husbands at home; for it is disgraceful for a woman to speak in the church. [Did the word of God originate with you? Or are you the only people it has reached?]

The digression gives a new meaning to the question that follows: "Did the word of God originate with you?" To whom is Paul speaking? To women?

Three Greek manuscripts—the codices Claromontanus (D 06), Augiensis (F 010), and Boernerianus (G 012)—render the passage not at this point (after 1 Cor 14:33) but at the end of the chapter, following 1 Cor 14:40. Evidently the text of their common ancestor-manuscript looks like the text example above. There are two possible explanations for the evidence: either the passage did not belong to the original text and was added later at different places, or the passage was moved to a better place because it was felt to interrupt the context. Both views could easily be supported by examples from New Testament manuscripts.[12]

But what is the connection to the context? Usually modern editors of the Bible tie this passage together with the preceding phrase: "As in all Christian congregations women should remain silent in church." The suggested connection is: If you do not want disorder but peace like all congregations then do not allow a woman to speak in church.

The Greek text in the extant manuscripts, however, does not give any clues as to where this sentence begins. The oldest Greek manuscripts do not have punctuation marks like commas and periods. Codex p46, for example, does not mark new paragraphs; it does not even give spaces between the words. The whole text of 1 Corinthians to a modern reader looks like one single, long word (plate 6).

The topic of women speaking at worship services does not fit the surrounding text very well. On the other hand the passage picks up very many words from the context: "instruct," "subject to the control," "speaking," "the churches." The expression "speaking women" loosely refers to the "speaking in tongues" of the prophets, using the word "speaking" with a negative connotation in regard to the women whereas it has a positive connotation in connection with "tongues."

In addition Paul seems to contradict himself. In a preceding passage Paul deals with the issue of women using their gift of prophecy during worship services. He seems to agree with this practice. All he asks is that women should wear something on their head while doing so.

> And every woman who prays or prophesies with her head uncovered dishonors her head—it is just as though her head were shaved.
>
>   1 Cor 11:5 (NIV)

PLATE 6 (opposite)
Chester Beatty Papyrus p46
The page covers the end of 1 Cor 14:34 and ends with 1 Cor 15:6. Of the preceding three lines of 1 Cor 14:34 two and a half lines are missing, leaving only eleven characters. At the top of the page the page number 110 is given in Greek letters. Someone added a few marks, probably to structure the text for correct reading, but did not do so very systematically. In line 18 the scribe had originally left some space. He probably wanted to fill in something he did not understand in the manuscript he copied, but later he decided that there was nothing to add there and he filled the empty space with a line. The following word as well was superfluous and the scribe put dots above each letter to indicate the deletion.[13]

ρι

ΚΑΘΩϹΚΑΙΟΝΟΜΟϹΛΕΓΕΙ ΕΙΔΕΤΙΜΑ
ΘΕΙΝ ΘΕΛΟΥϹΙΝ ΕΝΟΙΚΩΤΟΥϹΙΔΙΟΥϹ
ΑΝΔΡΑϹ ΕΠΕΡΩΤΑΤΩϹΑΝ ΑΙϹΧΡΟΝ
ΓΑΡΓΥΝΑΙΚΙΛΑΛΕΙΝ ΕΝΕΚΚΛΗϹΙΑ
ΗΑΦΥΜΩΝ Ο ΛΟΓΟϹΤΟΥΘΥ
Η ΕΙϹΥΜΑϹΜΟΝΟΥϹ ΚΑΤΗΝΤΗϹΕΝ
ΕΙΤΙϹΔΟΚΕΙ ΠΡΟΦΗΤΗϹΕΙΝΑΙ ΗΠΝΕΥ
ΜΑΤΙΚΟϹ ΓΕΙΝΩϹΚΕΤΩΑΓΡΑΦΩ ΥΜΕΙΝ
ΟΤΙΚΥ ΕϹΤΙΝ ΕΝΤΟΛΗ ΕΙΔΕΤΙϹΑΓΝΟΕΙ
ΑΓΝΟΕΙΤΩ ΩϹΤΕ ΑΔΕΛΦΟΙ ΖΗΛΟΥΤΕ
ΤΟΠΡΟΦΗΤΕΥΕΙΝ ΚΑΙΛΑΛΕΙΝ ΜΗΚΩ
ΛΥΕΤΕ ΕΝΓΛΩϹϹΑΙϹΠΑΝΤΑΔΕΕΥϹΧΗ
ΜΟΝΩϹ ΚΑΙΚΑΤΑΤΑΞΙΝ ΓΕΙΝΕϹΘΩ
ΓΝΩΡΙΖΩΔΕΥΜΙΝΑΔΕΛΦΟΙΤΟΕΥΑΓ
ΓΕΛΙΟΝ Ο ΕΥΗΓΓΕΛΙϹΑΜΗΝΥΜΕΙΝ
Ο ΚΑΙΠΑΡΕΛΑΒΕΤΕ ΕΝΩΚΑΙΕϹΤΗΚΑΤΕ
ΔΙΟΥ ΚΑΙϹΩΖΕϹΘΕ ΤΙΝΙΛΟΓΩ ΕΥΗΓ
ΓΕΛΙϹΑΜΗΝΥΜΕΙΝ
ΚΑΤΕΧΕΙΝ ΕΙΚΑΤΕΧΕΤΕ ΕΚΤΟϹΕΙΜΗ
ΕΙΚΗ ΕΠΙϹΤΕΥϹΑΤΕ ΠΑΡΕΔΩΚΑΓΑΡ
ΥΜΕΙΝ ΕΝΠΡΩΤΟΙϹ Ο ΚΑΙΠΑΡΕΛΑΒΟΝ
ΟΤΙ ΧΡϹ ΑΠΕΘΑΝΕΝ ΥΠΕΡΤΩΝΑΜΑΡ
ΤΙΩΝΗΜΩΝ ΚΑΤΑΤΑϹΓΡΑΦΑϹ Κ
ΕΤΑΦΗ ΚΑΙΟΤΙ ΕΓΗΓΕΡΤΑΙ
ΤΗΤΡΙΤΗΗΜΕΡΑΤΑ
ωφθη κηφα δε

No matter how we explain passages like this, unexpected digressions are one of the characteristic features of the letters of Paul.

Inconsistency of Style

Another peculiarity about the letters of Paul is that some letters differ considerably in style from other letters. This inconsistency of style has especially been noted for Hebrews and the three letters 1–2 Timothy and Titus, which are usually called Pastoral letters. Word statistics show that the Pastoral letters provide 335 words not found in the other letters of Paul. Every letter, of course, has a certain number of unique words, but the proportion here is two and a half times higher than with the other letters of the collection. On the other hand, several phrases repeated more than once in the Pastoral letters are not used at all in the other letters. There are several short words in Greek that are not really necessary but convey writing habits the writer himself might not be aware of, for example as in English the use of "now," "of course," "really," or "actually." The other letters of Paul have many of these words, but the Pastoral letters are lacking them completely.[14]

Anachronisms

Several passages of the letters of Paul can easily be interpreted as anachronisms. An anachronism is a chronological misplacing of persons, objects, or events in regard to each other. If you watch a Western and see an Indian wearing a digital wrist watch, you are witnessing a blunt anachronism. Anachronisms usually are not intended by the author. Mistakes like this are sometimes the only clue to detect a faked document.

Now anachronisms can only be recognized if we have some reliable historical knowledge independent from the text that may contain the anachronism. And even then it still depends on how ready the interpreter is to concede that the author may want to cheat. Concerning the New Testament we are somewhat prejudiced. Which reader of the Bible would readily agree that an author of the New Testament would try to deceive his readers?

On the other hand, from the little we know of the early and middle second century from sources outside the New Testament, we are well informed about two major religious movements competing with what came to be catholic Christianity: Gnosticism and the church of Marcion. Both movements were very strong. Many Gnostics and all the members of the Marcionite Church considered themselves true Christians. The resemblance of the ideas described in the letter to the Colossians with Gnostic ideology is very close. If gnosis did not yet exist in the days of Paul then this would be a clear anachronism—Paul fighting a dangerous religious movement of the second century.

A well-known passage often interpreted as an anachronism is found at the end of the first letter to Timothy. The main book Marcion wrote was entitled *Antitheses*. Let me translate the Greek text literally:

> Timothy, guard what has been entrusted to your care. Turn away from godless chatter and from the *Antitheses* of what is falsely called *Gnosis*.
>
> 1 Tim 6:20

Both words have a second meaning. *Antitheses* is translated as "opposing ideas" in the NIV, and the Greek term *gnosis* means "knowledge." So the whole passage reads in the NIV: "Turn away from godless chatter and the opposing ideas of what is falsely called knowledge. . . .", and the NRSV translates: "Avoid the profane chatter and contradictions of what is falsely called knowledge." Nevertheless, a second-century Christian probably could not help but think of Marcion and Gnosticism when he read those lines, understanding the passage as a prophetical warning. Without doubt it was the official policy of the leaders of the catholic Christian Church, who promoted the canonical edition of the letters of Paul in the second century, to segregate from the Marcionite Church and from Gnosticism.

Another feature of this letter to Timothy is that Paul presupposes a structure of the churches including a bishop (1 Tim 3:1b-7), deacons (1 Tim 3:8-13), elders (1 Tim 5:17-22), and widows (1 Tim 5:3-16). This seems to reflect the ecclesiastical organization of the second century and not the situation in Paul's days.

Let us have a closer look at the widows, for example. In the second century the term widow covered more than just the depiction of a woman who had lost her husband. It represented a job description and was used for members of a Christian congregation who fulfilled a specific ministry.

> Greetings to the families of my brethren, including their wives and children, and to the virgins who are enrolled among the widows.
>
> *IgnSmyrn* 13:1[15]

When bishop Ignatius of Antioch wrote to the congregation in Smyrna (ca. 110 C.E.), it did not cause any difficulty either on his part or on the part of the addressee to refer to "virgins"—women who had never married—as "widows." If you have a look at 1 Tim 5:9-10 now, you will immediately realize that this passage is not speaking of women who have lost their husbands.

> No widow may be put on the list of widows unless she is over sixty, has been faithful to her husband, and is well known for her good deeds, such as bringing up children, showing hospitality, washing the feet of the saints, helping those in trouble and devoting herself to all kinds of good deeds.   1 Tim 5:9-10 (NIV)

To be a widow in the sense of 1 Timothy a woman's name had to be kept on a list, and one qualified for this list only under clearly defined conditions, such as age limit, sexual behavior, bringing up children successfully, and other moral and social qualities. To many interpreters of the New Testament this looks like a plain anachronism; it describes Paul solving problems that did not exist until many decades after his death.

Competing Theories of Interpretation

The characteristics of the letters of Paul that I have just described are susceptible to many different interpretations.

Traditional View

Traditionally all the letters of Paul are understood as authentic letters, written by the apostle and handed down to us essentially looking like the letters Paul mailed to the designated addresses without having undergone any substantial editorial changes. They were written at a specific date and place, usually because Paul could not personally visit the addressed person or congregation. The Greek manuscripts of the Authorized Byzantine Version recorded an old tradition about where Paul wrote the letters. The Geneva Bible, the English translation brought to North America on the Mayflower by the Pilgrims, and most editions of the King James Version, both translate the short subscriptions preserved in the Authorized Byzantine Version. The notes of the Geneva New Testament (1560) to the first four letters read:[16]

Following Rom 16:27
Written to the Romanes from Corinthus, and sent by Phebe, seruant of the Church, which is at Cenchrea.

Following 1 Cor 16:24
The first Epistle to the Corinthians, written from Philippi, and sent by Stephanas, and Fortunatus, and Achaicus, and Timotheus.

Following 2 Cor 13:13
The second Epistle to the Corinthians, written from Philippi, a citie in Macedonia, and sent by Titus and Lucas.

Following Gal 6:18
Vnto the Galatians written from Rome.

The place given for 1 Corinthians is probably wrong, for as we have seen, Paul was in Ephesus when he wrote 1 Cor 16:8-9, and there is no clear reference in the text of Galatians to suggest Rome as the place where Paul wrote that letter. Nevertheless, the uniformity of these subscriptions persists to this day, and although they did not have much influence on historical research, they formed the consciousness of readers of the Bible for many centuries, promoting the traditional view that the letters of Paul represent single letters taken from his personal correspondence.

But the traditional view has been challenged throughout the history of Christian Bible interpretation.

Authenticity

The Christian theologian Clement of Alexandria, who taught in Alexandria at the end of the second century C.E., explained the difference of style of the letter to the Hebrews in comparison with other letters of Paul this way: Paul wrote the epistle anonymously in Hebrew and Luke translated it into Greek.[17] But another explanation became very popular among Christian exegetes at the same time. Only a few years later the famous church father and brilliant scholar, Origen, who died in 254, reports:

> That the character of the diction of the epistle entitled To the Hebrews has not the apostle's rudeness in speech, who confessed himself *rude in speech* (reference to 2 Cor 11:6), that is, in style, but that the epistle is better Greek in the framing of its diction, will be admitted by everyone who is able to discern differences of style. . . . Yet the account which has reached us [is twofold], some saying that Clement, who was bishop of the Romans, wrote the epistle, others, that it was Luke, he who wrote the Gospel and the Acts.[18]   Eusebius, *H.E.* 6:25:11.14

As early as the second century the Pauline authorship of Hebrews was questioned by interpreters of the New Testament. This skepticism has been passed on over the centuries, and today only seven of the fourteen letters of Paul are held to be genuine by most New Testament scholars: Romans, 1–2 Corinthians, Galatians, Philippians, 1 Thessalonians, and Philemon. There is no consensus of opinion among scholars about the authenticity of the other seven letters: Ephesians, Colossians, 2 Thessalonians, Hebrews, 1–2 Timothy, and Titus. Differences of style and passages interpreted as anachronisms are the main arguments used to support this view.

Letter-Compositions

Another attempt to interpret characteristic features of the letters of Paul is to understand them as letter-compositions. That is to say, one letter is a composite from material of more than one authentic letter. This view is very popular for Romans, where Romans 16 is held to be a separate letter, and for 2 Corinthians and has been proposed for other letters as well. This interpretation accounts for the evident changes of attitude and tries to understand the unexpected digressions as parts of the missing letters mentioned in the context.

Literary Letters

Another explanation is that the letters of Paul are not real letters; they are literature, to be read aloud in worship services—speeches clad in the dress of a letter. Their literary character is related to literary testaments and farewell speeches. Paul wrote down the essence of his message for Christian generations to come. The specific address is not essential, and the specific occasion—where, when, and why Paul wrote the letter—is not important and might even be fictional.[19]

Treating the letters of Paul as literary letters helps us understand the uniform beginning of the letters, especially the wish for grace and peace in the salutation and the following expression of thanks to God. These characteristics can be paralleled much better in pieces of literature than in private letters. Specific information that is of interest only to the addressee of the original letter—like greetings, plans, and specific requests—is typical for private correspondences. This implies, however, that the letters described above, which lack this kind of information, fit the picture of literary letters very well. Autographic subscriptions and the reference to letters missing in the collection indicate features of an incomplete private correspondence. These passages are held to be fictional if we understand the letters as literary letters. Unexpected digressions, inconsistency of style, and anachronisms could document later editorial activity and therefore indicate literary letters.

The sudden changes of attitude in 2 Corinthians present a problem for both views. They indicate that parts of 2 Corinthians were written at different occasions and that 2 Corinthians therefore does not represent the text of one single private letter. On the other hand, if we view 2 Corinthians as a piece of literature, we will have to explain why an author or editor would tie contradicting passages like that together.

Summary

These views differ considerably in their idea of the amount and the character of editorial work put into the text of the letters of Paul before they were published in the canonical edition. This is what we will investigate in the following chapter. What kind of editorial changes would editors make in antiquity when they prepared letters for publication?

3

Interpreting the Letters of Paul in the Light of Ancient Letter Collections

Compatible Collections

Linus comes home from Church School and meets Charlie Brown.

"Where have you been?" Charlie Brown asks.

"Church school. We've been studying the letters of the Apostle Paul," Linus answers.

"That should be interesting."

"It is—although I must admit it makes me feel a little guilty."

"Why?"

Linus replies: "I always feel like I am reading someone else's mail!"[20]

I told this story to my students during a lecture. They roared with laughter. I had expected some smiles, but this hilarious reaction came as a surprise to me. Then I asked the students if they thought that the letters of Paul were real letters. Is the text we now read the text of the letter Paul mailed to the addressed men and women? Practically all of them thought it was.

No doubt most of us would feel uneasy reading someone else's mail. So what makes us laugh at the naive reaction of the little boy? I think the reason is that we read these letters in the midst of other writings in a book we refer to as the New Testament. As soon as letters are published, they cease to be private letters, no matter how private they originally might have been. The reader of the published letter is a different person from the addressee of the original letter. The literary character of the letter changes.

Literary or Private Letters

Let us stop for a moment and get our terminology straight. What exactly is a private letter and what is a literary letter? If I use the term *private letter*, I think of a letter written because the author was not able or not willing to speak directly to the addressed person. As soon as the letter reaches its destination and is read by the addressee, the main function of the letter is fulfilled.

A literary letter has other goals. It is a piece of art. In it the author may try to write down his philosophy, as the Latin philosopher and contemporary of Paul, L. Annaeus Seneca (4 B.C.E.–65 C.E.), did in his *Epistulae morales*. Another author may give his poems the form of love letters as the first-century poet P. Ovidius Naso (43 B.C.E.–18 C.E.) did in his *Ars amatoria*. Another may simply put down easy-to-read entertainment, as the Roman politician C. Plinius Caecilius Secundus (61/62–ca. 112 C.E.) did in his nine books of letters.

Mailed or Not? The distinguishing mark of a private letter in contrast to a literary letter is the answer to the question, Did the letter necessarily have to be sent in order to fulfill its purpose? If the answer is "yes" then it is to be regarded as a private letter. But if a letter could just as well be handed to the addressee by the author and still fulfill its purpose it should not be called private.

Let me give you two examples. A letter written by a child to the president of the United States, asking him to make peace, published in the local daily newspaper at the same time it was mailed, could just as well be handed to the President by the child. It therefore is not a private letter. Many literary letters have a fictive author and a fictive address. It is impossible to deliver them.

The other example is taken from the Bible.

> Many have undertaken to draw up an account of the things that have been fullfilled among us. . . . Therefore, since I myself have carefully investigated everything from the beginning, it seemed good also to me to write an orderly account for you, most excellent Theophilus, so that you may know the certainty of the things you have been taught.
>
> Luke 1:1, 3-4 (NIV)

The first sentences of the Gospel of Luke give the name of the addressed person, Theophilus. This makes it look like a letter. Clearly the Gospel of Luke is a piece of literature, not a private letter. One could easily imagine the author of the Gospel writing this account and then personally handing the first copy to Theophilus. Maybe Theophilus is even a name the author made up. The literal translation of Theophilus is "the one who loves God." This would fit for every Christian reader of the Gospel.

Original or Copy? The other distinguishing mark is that a private
letter is always an original. As soon as it is copied and distributed to
persons other than the addressee, it ceases to be a private letter. A
literary letter is always a copy. Under this aspect the observation that
the letters of Paul provide traces of autographic subscriptions is of
great importance. They inform the reader that his text is a copy of an
original document. These autographic passages are evident only in
the original. They cannot be reproduced. On the other hand, it is
obvious that the canonical edition of the letters of Paul was produced to be copied for public use and therefore has to be regarded
as a collection of literary letters.

I investigated about two hundred letter collections from 300 B.C.E.
to around 400 C.E., written by more than one hundred different
authors, covering more than three thousand letters. I concentrated
my studies on letter collections that claim to preserve material from
private correspondences. They seemed to me to be the most ade-
quate material for a comparison with the letters of Paul.

In the following I will refer to published letter collections that
preserve authentic private letters as "compatible collections."

Three Stages of Development

I asked the letter collections I examined the same question over and
over again: What kind of editorial changes would editors make in
antiquity when they prepared letters for publication? The most
important thing I learned was that letter collections do not just
happen. They develop. Usually three stages can be recognized, and
at each stage different editorial goals are pursued (table 6).

TABLE 6
Three Stages of Development

1. Authorized Recensions
   The author of the letter prepares letters for publication.
2. Expanded Editions
   After the author's death these editions are expanded. Further editions of
   published and unpublished letters are produced.
3. Comprehensive Editions
   All the available editions are combined.

The first stage is that most of the letter collections using materials
from authentic private letters originated with the author of the letters.
The author himself was responsible for the selection of letters and

for editing them. If this publication was a success, often further letter collections would follow. I will refer to these editions as "authorized recensions."

The second stage begins when the author dies. Unpublished letters are collected. If their topic is somehow related to authorized recensions, they are published as appendices to these collections. Otherwise letters covering the same subject or addressed to the same person are put together and published as separate volumes. I will call editions of this second stage "expanded editions."

In the third stage of the development of a letter collection scribes try to produce manuscripts containing all known letters. I will refer to editions of this third stage as "comprehensive editions."

Let me relate these three stages to the letters of Paul. Manuscripts containing all fourteen letters evidently represent the stage of comprehensive editions. That was easy. But what about older editions?

We have already noted that collections without Hebrews existed, which contained only thirteen letters of Paul. Does the thirteen-letter collection document an expanded edition of the second stage? And if so, is it still possible to tell which letters might have belonged to the edition authorized by Paul? I believe that the Greek text of the letters of Paul as it is preserved in the manuscripts provides enough clues to answer both questions.

Before presenting the result of my research on compatible letter collections and interpreting the canonical edition of the letters of Paul on this background, the question has to be asked whether the letters of Paul, although they are now part of the Bible, were produced and reproduced very much the same way as most of the other letter collections of that time (especially in view of the fact that Paul is not a pagan writer but one of the authors of the New Testament)? Could it not be that the letters of Paul originated in a unique and unparalleled way for which there are no analogies?

It is possible. If you hold that point of view anything I will say from now on is worthless to you. This is the risk of any historical research, however, not only of Biblical Studies. All we have to argue with are analogies. All we can do is to describe what is most likely to have happened. Historical judgment is based on an evaluation of probability. And if we have to do with unique events, most methods of historical criticism fail.

I do not think that the letters of Paul originated in a very spectacular way. The evidence fits the picture of other letter collections too well. So if you are interested in an interpretation that fits the evidence, you are invited to walk with me and to criticize any of my steps. I am confident that this path brings us closer to the historical truth. The only alternative I see is to say nothing at all.

Sequence of Letters

As long as book production could rely only on handwritten copies, rearrangement of older collections was a very unpopular and difficult technical task. Manuscript tradition proves again and again that collections preserve the order of their writings with great persistence. This is especially true for letter collections. When new letters were added to an older collection, editors usually would put the new letters at the end of the collection. They would not rearrange the older collection. If, for example, the letters were dated and the older collection was arranged chronologically, the new letters would not be placed between the letters of the older collection according to their date. The new letters would be added at the end in an appendix. But—and this is a most important observation—the letters of the appendix would be arranged chronologically. Therefore, the beginning of the appendix is marked by the first letter, which does not match the chronological order. And the analysis is confirmed if all following letters are arranged according to their date.

I could say it in a more general way: Once the principle of arrangement of the older collection is established, the beginning of the appendix is marked by a letter that does not match this principle. The beginning of an appendix is confirmed if from that letter on, all following letters are arranged again according to the principle of arrangement of the older collection.

Principle of Arrangement

So what we have to do is to find the principle of arrangement of the letters of Paul. As I have shown above, the letters of Paul are arranged according to their addresses into two parts: the letters to congregations and the letters to individuals. But what is the principle within these two groups?

It is the length of the texts of the letters (table 7).

TABLE 7
The Approximate Length of the Letters of Paul

	Characters	*Percentage*		*Difference*[21]
Rom	34,410	18.4		0
1 Cor	32,767	17.5	-	1,643
2 Cor	22,280	11.9	-	10,487
Gal	11,091	5.9	-	11,189
Eph	12,012	6.4	+	921
Phil	8,009	4.3	-	4,003
Col	7,897	4.2	-	112
1 Thess	7,423	4.0	-	474
2 Thess	4,055	2.2	-	3,368
1 Tim	8,869	4.7	+	4,814
2 Tim	6,538	3.5	-	2,331
Titus	3,733	2.0	-	2,805
Phlm	1,575	0.8	-	2,158
Heb	26,382	14.1		
TOTAL	187,041			

The beginning of the second part, the letters to individuals, is confirmed by the data. With 1 Timothy the principle of arrangement is repeated because 1 Timothy is longer than 2 Thessalonians. The letters to congregations, however, are not arranged strictly according to their length. Ephesians is longer than Galatians by more than 900 characters. But the letters following Galatians—Ephesians, Philippians, Colossians, 1–2 Thessalonians—are arranged again according to their length. Thus, Ephesians does not match the established principle of arrangement, but following this very letter all letters comply to the principle of arrangement again. Ephesians therefore seems to mark the beginning of an appendix.

Other Explanations? Let us challenge this analysis. Could it be that the difference between the length of Galatians and Ephesians is so small that the editors did not realize it? Could the sequence better be explained as a mistake?

Two arguments can meet this objection. The letter to the Colossians is a little more than 100 characters shorter than Philippians.

The difference between the letter to the Galatians and the letter to the Ephesians with more than 900 characters is eight times as large. Why would an editor correctly figure the length of Colossians and Philippians, but not the length of Ephesians and Galatians?

The second argument is the clear evidence that editors were very well aware of the length of text. Scribes had developed sophisticated methods to determine the exact length. This was important for all professionals in the book business because the length of the text determined the price of the book. In many manuscripts—p46, Codex Vaticanus (B 03), Codex Sinaiticus (ℵ 01), and Codex Claromontanus (D 06)—the length of the text was noted by the scribe at the end of each letter or in a separate list. Therefore, it is very unlikely that the sequence of Ephesians following Galatians is the result of a mistake.

Conclusion

Judging from the evidence of other letter collections, Ephesians indicates the beginning of an appendix to an authorized recension of Romans, 1–2 Corinthians, Galatians. If this analysis is correct, Romans, 1–2 Corinthians, and Galatians are to be treated as a literary unit. It is highly probable that this old collection was edited and prepared for publication by Paul himself. After his death, more letters were added to this authorized recension. The thirteen-letter collection represents this stage, an expanded edition of the letters of Paul.[22]

The following chapters will interpret the first four letters of Paul as a unit. They shall demonstrate that this theory helps better to understand characteristic features of the letters of Paul.

4

Paul's Authorized Recension of the Letter to the Romans, the Two Letters to the Corinthians, and the Letter to the Galatians

I shall interpret the first four letters of the canonical edition as the relic of Paul's authorized recension of these letters. To do this we shall proceed in four steps.

First we shall have a look at typical editorial activity regarding ancient letter collections. Second we will apply these findings to Paul. The third step is to investigate the literary genre of the letter to the Romans, the Corinthian correspondence, and the letter to the Galatians. Last but not least we will sum up the evidence that helps us understand Paul's intention when he edited his letters.

Typical Editorial Changes

What kind of editing is to be expected when an author prepares his own letters for publication? The ideal situation in finding an answer would be to have the original letter as it was sent and compare it to the published letter. I do not know of any letter in antiquity where this is possible. There are other ways, however, to shed some light on the editorial activity of the author.

Some authors tell us about the editorial changes they made before they allowed their letters to be published. The Roman politician and famous orator, Marcus Tullius Cicero, wrote to his publisher Atticus in a letter dated July 9, 44 B.C., one year before he died:

> So far there is no collection of my letters. But Tiro has about seventy now. And some more will have to be taken from you. But I still will have to go over them and correct them. Then they might be published.[23]   *AdAtt* 16:5:5

55

Selection

The first thing the author has to do is to select letters. Cicero's comments show how carefully he proceeded. He mentions 70 letters. No less than 774 letters of Cicero have survived to this day, and there is decisive proof of the existence of at least 17 more ancient collections of his letters that have been lost.[24]

Cicero evidently had copies of some of the letters he wanted to publish, but he thought of asking Atticus to return a few letters Cicero had written to him. This sheds some light on the situation of an author willing to publish part of his private correspondence. For Cicero it was natural to keep a copy of some of the letters he wrote in his personal archives, but he did not keep copies of all his letters. The Latin writer Cornelius Nepos describes a visit to the archives where Cicero kept his correspondence with Atticus.[25] In ancient days it often happened that for some reason a letter written later arrived earlier. (A famous example is Augustine's letter ep 28 to Jerome, written in 395 from Hippo in North Africa, which reached Jerome in Bethlehem eight years later, after Jerome had received and answered several other letters from Augustine.) Some of the letter collections published after Cicero's death are arranged in the chronological order in which they arrived at their destination and not in the chronological order in which they were written. This order of the letters suggests that the collections published were taken from the archives of the addressees and not from Cicero's.

Why did Cicero choose only 70 letters? The collection he talks about in his letter to Atticus is still extant. It forms the thirteenth book of the letters to his Family, usually referred to as *AdFam 13*. This collection comprises exclusively letters of recommendation Cicero wrote for friends. They are rhetoric masterpieces, bearing witness of Cicero's excellent style, his high education, fine taste, and persuading arguments.

Editing

Shortly after the publication of this letter collection Cicero was assassinated. After Cicero's death his slave and secretary Tiro proceeded to publish additional letters. This creates an interesting situation. We have letters edited by Cicero and letters not edited by him. A comparison of both allows us to get an idea of the amount and character of editorial work Cicero put into his letters before he allowed them to be published. The difference is striking. In 1345 the Italian Renaissance poet Francesco Petrarch was the first to rediscover the letters of Cicero in an old manuscript after they had been unknown for centuries. When he read them, he was shocked and disappointed— shocked because of the colloquial language and bad style of the letters and disappointed because the letters revealed a politician full of intrigue, whose poor character surpassed by far his bad grammar.[26]

Names

An author would be expected to be keenly aware of the names of people still living. There is a strong editorial tendency to delete all names that are unimportant to the reader of the collection.

For example, Bishop Cyprian of Carthage, who died in 258 as a martyr, published several collections of his letters himself. Some of the official letters which he wrote together with other bishops still provide all the names. For example, the letter referred to in modern editions as ep 70 (*ep* stands for *epistula*, the Latin expression for letter), gives the names of all 31 bishops who wrote the letter together with Cyprian and the names of the 18 addressed bishops. This was the proper way to begin an official letter. On the other hand, many letters of the collection leave out the names. Ep 64 begins, "Cyprian and the other 66 colleagues who took part in the council greet brother Fidus." Ep 61 reads, "Cyprian together with his colleagues greets brother Lucius," and ep 72 starts out, "Cyprian and the others greet Stephanus." This editorial tendency to delete greetings that are of no great importance to the reader of the collection is typical for any first edition of private letters, whether the author himself or someone else prepared them for publication.

But it is not only the greetings that are affected. Another important aspect of names of people contemporary to the author is that the text usually reflects their relationship to the author. Relationships can change. There are several cases in antiquity when an author reedited one of his books and prepared a second edition. Sure enough, he would usually go over the personal passages and correct them if necessary. He would strike out an originally friendly comment about someone who in the meantime had become his enemy.

For example, Jerome was one of the most brilliant biblical scholars of the fourth century; in fact, he is the editor of the Vulgate, the Latin Bible still used today. As a young man he shared a deep friendship with his well-known colleague Rufinus and their mutual friend, lady Melania. In a book on the history of the Christian church Jerome dedicated a chapter to the virtues of Rufinus and Melania. By the time he updated the book to prepare a second edition, however, the friendship had broken; Jerome and Rufinus had become adversaries. Jerome deleted the passage. Rufinus himself mentions the deletion in one of his books.[27] This practice of deleting names because the positive or negative connotation was not thought to be acceptable to the reader is referred to as *damnatio memoriae.*

When Paul prepared an edition of his letters, he was very much in the position of an author preparing a second edition. The letters had been written some time ago. The situation had changed. People he had referred to in a friendly way in the original letters might have become enemies in the meantime.

Specific Information

Information valid only for a short period of time is typical for private letters. Very often this kind of information is the main reason for writing. For the public, those reasons usually are not of great interest and an editor might easily deem them unnecessary to reproduce.

Summary

In preparing letters for publication, an author would first of all make a selection. He would either have copies of the letters he sent or he would ask the addressee to send him the originals. Then we would expect him to work on his style. He would try to be as precise as possible. He might be aware of misunderstandings he did not think of when he wrote the original letter. He would carefully check the references to living persons and he would be likely to delete trivial passages that do not contribute to the task of the collection, such as greetings or travel plans.

Understanding Paul
as an Editor

How do these findings apply to Paul's authorized recension?

I love detective stories. And there is one thing we can learn from Sherlock Holmes, Lord Peter Wimsey, Hercule Poirot, and Perry Mason: the little, trivial observations often provide the most useful information. The comparison with other letter collections has shown that this is exactly what we will have to do—look at the greetings, travel plans, names of persons and places mentioned, and other seemingly trivial information.

Greetings

Let us look first at the greetings. Greetings are passages we would expect an editor to abbreviate when preparing a private correspondence for publication.

> The churches in the province of Asia send you greetings. Aquila and Priscilla greet you warmly in the Lord, and so does the church that meets at their house. All the brothers here send you greetings. Greet one another with a holy kiss. I, Paul, write this greeting in my own hand.   1 Cor 16:19-21 (NIV)

> Greet one another with a holy kiss. All the saints send their greetings.
>   2 Cor 13:12 (NIV)

Galatians has no greeting at all, 1 Corinthians mentions two persons by name, Aquila and Priscilla, but, other than that, it ends like 2 Corinthians with a very general greeting. This matches exactly the evidence in other compatible letter collections, where greetings are abbreviated.

The evidence in Romans is different. In Romans 16 no less than 32 persons or parties are greeted, and eight people send their personal regards.

> I commend to you our sister (1) Phoebe. . . . Greet: (2) Priscilla (3) Aquila (4) the church that meets in their house (5) Epenetus, who was the first convert to Christ in the province of Asia (6) Mary (7) Andronicus (8) Junia (9) Ampliatus (10) Urbanus (11) Stachys (12) Apelles (13) those who belong to the household of Aristobulus (14) Herodion (15) those who are in the household of Narcissus who are in the Lord (16) Tryphena (17) Tryphosa (18) Persis (19) Rufus (20) Rufus' mother (21) Asyncritus (22) Phlegon (23) Hermes (24) Patrobas (25) Hermas (26) the brothers with them (27) Philologus (28) Julia (29) Nereus (30) his sister (31) Olympas (32) all the saints with them. . . .
>   Rom 16:1-16a

> All the churches of Christ send greetings . . . (1) Timothy (2) Lucius (3) Jason (4) Sosipater (5) Tertius (6) Gaius (7) Erastus (8) Quartus.
>   Rom 16:16b-23

Summary. As I pointed out above comparing the letters of Paul with other ancient letter collections, it is very natural for an author to sum up greetings when he prepares his letters for publication. It is not the omission of the greetings that has to be explained in Galatians and 1–2 Corinthians; rather, an explanation has to be found for the numerous personal greetings Paul left in his letter to the Romans.

Names

The remainder of Romans is even more surprising in that so many names appear in the final passages of this letter. Not a single person is mentioned in the first 15 chapters of Romans by name. Before we consider different explanations for this observation, let us look at the use of proper names in the other three letters.

1 Corinthians. Not counting Paul, in 1 Corinthians fourteen persons are mentioned by name: (1) Sosthenes 1:1, (2) Chloe 1:11, (3) Apollos 1:12; 3:4.5.6.22; 4:6; 16:12, (4) Cephas 1:12; 3:22; 9:5; 15:5, (5) Crispus 1:14, (6) Gaius 1:14, (7) Stephanas 1:16; 16:15.17, (8) Timothy 4:17; 16:10, (9) Barnabas 9:6, (10) James 15:7, (11) Fortunatus 16:17, (12) Achaicus 16:17, (13) Aquila 16:19, (14) Priscilla 16:19.

One striking difference between 1 Corinthians and Romans is that in 1 Corinthians the names are not restricted to the greetings. As we have already observed, the greetings are very global, mentioning only Aquila and Priscilla by name. Let us have a look at the other names, one by one:

> I rejoice at the coming of Stephanas and Fortunatus and Achaicus, because they have made up for your absence; for they refreshed my spirit as well as yours. So give recognition to such persons.
>
> 1 Cor 16:17 (NRSV)

> For it has been reported to me by Chloe's people that there are quarrels among you, my brothers and sisters.   1 Cor 1:11 (NRSV)

Fortunatus and Achaicus are closely connected to Stephanas. These three men are introduced by Paul as his source of information (1 Cor 16:17). Another group of visitors Paul refers to are persons from Chloe's household (1 Cor 1:11). So these four names are well introduced. When writing to people you have not seen for a considerable period of time it makes sense to tell them where you got some new information. Sosthenes functions as coauthor and therefore has to be mentioned by name. Apollo, Cephas, and Timothy are mentioned more than once and at substantial places in the letter. Together with Barnabas and James these five are among the circle of prominent Christians probably most readers had heard of and for this reason their names were not deleted. This leaves us with two names, Gaius and Crispus.

> I am thankful that I did not baptize any of you except Crispus and Gaius, so no one can say that you were baptized into my name. (Yes, I also baptized the household of Stephanas; beyond that, I don't remember if I baptized anyone else.) 1 Cor 1:14-16 (NIV)

Paul argues that as a rule "Christ did not send me to baptize, but to preach the gospel" (1 Cor 1:17). To strengthen his argument he gives all the exceptions to the rule he remembers. Trying to be complete at this point he mentions names that are of no great importance to the reader of his letter collection.

The way persons are introduced in 1 Corinthians is different from the evidence in Romans 16; the persons mentioned by name play a specific role in the literary context of 1 Corinthians.

2 Corinthians. 2 Corinthians does not contain any proper names besides Paul, Timothy, who serves as coauthor of the letter (2 Cor 1:1), Silas (2 Cor 1:19), Titus (2 Cor 2:13; 7:6.13.14; 8:6.16.23; 12:18), and King Aretas (2 Cor 11:32), definitely a well-known man at that time.

It is quite clear that Paul's letters to the Corinthians originally must have had some kind of personal greetings that are now missing. And 2 Corinthians preserves another passage where it seems obvious that a proper name was deleted. Together with Titus, Paul sends a brother "who is praised by all the churches for his service to the gospel." But he does not give his name.

> I thank God, who put into the heart of Titus the same concern I have for you. For Titus not only welcomed our appeal, but he is coming to you with much enthusiasm and on his own initiative. And we are sending along with him the brother who is praised by all the churches for his service to the gospel. What is more, he was chosen by the churches to accompany us as we carry the offering, which we administer in order to honor the Lord himself and to show our eagerness to help. 2 Cor 8:16-19 (NIV)

Besides the obvious fact that it does not make much sense to write a letter of recommendation for someone and not give his name, there are six comparable passages in the canonical edition of the letters of Paul (1 Cor 4:17; 1 Thess 3:2-5; Phil 2:19-23; Phil 2:25-30; Eph 6:21-22; Col 4:7-9) that turn the argument into a decisive proof. In these passages Paul sends one of his fellow workers. The passages all have very much the same structure, and they all contain the name of the person to be sent. That the missing name is not just to be seen as a singular accident of text tradition but as a deliberate deletion is confirmed by the second mention of the ominous brother accompanying Titus. There too the name is missing.

> I urged Titus to go to you and I sent our *brother* with him.
>
> 2 Cor 12:18a (NIV)

Authors delete names when preparing their letters for a broader audience for two reasons. Either the names are of no interest to the addressee of the collection because they do not know the people, or, if they know the name, the connotation has changed. The first possibility is unlikely because Paul introduces the brother with the words "who is praised by all the churches" and therefore presupposes that the brother was probably well known. Consequently this would mean that the brother mentioned here with praise is no longer a friend of Paul's at the time he edited 2 Corinthians.

Galatians. In Galatians the names of five prominent Christian leaders are given—the apostles John and Peter, James, the brother of Jesus, the missionary Barnabas, and Paul's co-worker Titus. Peter, Barnabas, and Titus had already been mentioned in the Corinthian correspondence. All five men play an essential role in the events Paul describes in Galatians. Mentioning their names does not constitute the kind of information pertinent for only a short period of time so characteristic for private letters.

Summary. After looking at proper names in the letter to the Romans, 1–2 Corinthians, and the letter to the Galatians, what it boils down to is to find an explanation for the list of greetings in Romans 16, and the greeting of Aquila and Priscilla in 1 Corinthians 16.

Travel Plans

As we have seen, one of the difficulties in understanding the letters of Paul as literary letters in contrast to private letters is the personal greetings. The other difficulty mentioned was information on plans and visits that had already taken place by the time the letters were edited. Because this type of information seems of no value to later

readers as we have noted, to delete it would be the normal proce-
dure. If it is not deleted, it is left there on purpose.

Let us again take a look at the whole collection of Romans, 1–2
Corinthians, and Galatians with this in mind, looking for information
pertinent only for a short period of time.

Galatians. The letter to the Galatians has no such information at all
and therefore should not cause any difficulties.

1 Corinthians, 2 Corinthians. The situation is very different within
the Corinthian correspondence. Paul announces that he "will come
. . . very soon" (1 Cor 4:18) to Corinth, but this announcement is
carefully embedded in the immediate context and cannot easily be
removed. There are no details given concerning how he plans to
travel or when he plans to arrive. This information might have been
deleted by Paul.

> Some of you have become arrogant, as if I were not coming to you.
> But I will come to you very soon, if the Lord is willing, and then I will
> find out not only how these arrogant people are talking, but what
> power they have. For the kingdom of God is not a matter of talk but
> of power. What do you prefer? Shall I come to you with a whip, or in
> love and with a gentle spirit?   1 Cor 4:18-21 (NIV)

Paul mentions travel plans at the end of 1 Corinthians. And this
time he goes into more detail, writing about his plans to visit Corinth
by way of Macedonia.

> Then, when I arrive, I will give letters of introduction to the men you
> approve and send them with your gift to Jerusalem. If it seems advis-
> able for me to go also, they will accompany me.
>   After I go through Macedonia, I will come to you—for I will be
> going through Macedonia. Perhaps I will stay with you awhile, or even
> spend the winter, so that you can help me on my journey, wherever I
> go. I do not want to see you now and make only a passing visit; I hope
> to spend some time with you, if the Lord permits. But I will stay on at
> Ephesus until Pentecost, because a great door for effective work has
> opened to me, and there are many who oppose me.
>   1 Cor 16:3-9 (NIV)

2 Corinthians provides firsthand information about Paul's
unpleasant experiences after he left Ephesus.

We do not want you to be uninformed, brothers, about the hardships

we suffered in the province of Asia. We were under great pressure, far
beyond our ability to endure, so that we despaired even of life.

2 Cor 1:8 (NIV)

Because I was confident of this, I planned to visit you first so that you
might benefit twice. I planned to visit you on my way to Macedonia
and to come back to you from Macedonia, and then to have you send
me on my way to Judea. When I planned this, did I do it lightly? Or
do I make my plans in a worldly manner so that in the same breath I
say, "Yes, yes" and "No, no"?   2 Cor 1:15-17 (NIV)

Note the location of Ephesus, Troas, Macedonia, and Corinth on
the map. These are the major stopovers of Paul's itinerary. In routing
Paul's journey it becomes clear why he says "So that you might
benefit twice" (2 Cor 1:15).

Paul evidently changed his itinerary. Originally he had planned to
travel from Ephesus to Corinth, go to Macedonia, and come back
to Corinth again. This way he could have stayed with them twice on
this journey. But then he decided to stick to the itinerary of
1 Corinthians 16—to travel from Ephesus, probably via Troas, to
Macedonia, and from there to Corinth. He was aware that this would
cause some disagreement on the side of the Corinthians. He must
have informed them about his plans, and now he excuses himself
for not coming as he had originally promised. The next city Paul
mentions is Troas.

Now when I went to Troas to preach the gospel of Christ and found
that the Lord had opened a door for me, I still had no peace of mind,
because I did not find my brother Titus there. So I said good-by to
them and went on to Macedonia.   2 Cor 2:12-13 (NIV)

Troas, like Ephesus, was part of the Roman province of Asia and
was the nearest seaport for travel from the northwestern area of this
province to Europe. Although Paul does not explicitly tell us where
exactly "in the province Asia" he "suffered the hardships" (2 Cor
1:8), it is safe to assume that he is talking about events related to his
trip from Ephesus to Troas. Paul proceeded with his journey as he
planned it in 1 Corinthians 16. He probably boarded a ship in Troas
and left for Macedonia.

Paul goes on to describe what happened in Macedonia. Macedonia is not a city. It is a region. Thessalonica and Philippi for
example are two Macedonian cities. But Paul does not mention any
specific city in 2 Corinthians. Instead, he recounts that at some point

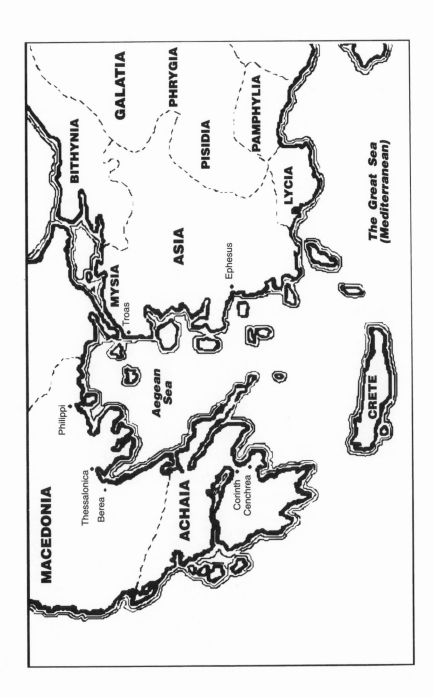

during his stay in Macedonia he met Titus again and received new information about the Corinthians.

> For when we came into Macedonia, this body of ours had no rest, but we were harassed at every turn—conflicts on the outside, fears within. But God, who comforts the downcast, comforted us by the coming of Titus, and not only by his coming but also by the comfort you had given him. He told us about your longing for me, your deep sorrow, your ardent concern for me, so that my joy was greater than ever.
>
> 2 Cor 7:5-13 (NIV)

The next piece of information Paul gives the reader of 2 Corinthians is that he sent Titus back to Corinth with the mission to organize the collection. Titus was accompanied by another brother, whose name Paul evidently deleted.

> So we urged Titus, since he had earlier made a beginning, to bring also to completion this act of grace on your part.   2 Cor 8:6 (NIV)

> I thank God, who put into the heart of Titus the same concern I have for you. For Titus not only welcomed our appeal, but he is coming to you with much enthusiasm and on his own initiative. And we are sending along with him the brother who is praised by all the churches for his service to the gospel. What is more, he was chosen by the churches to accompany us as we carry the offering, which we administer in order to honor the Lord himself and to show our eagerness to help.   2 Cor 8:16-19 (NIV)

> Did I exploit you through any of the men I sent you? I urged Titus to go to you and I sent our brother with him. Titus did not exploit you, did he? Did we not act in the same spirit and follow the same course?
>
> 2 Cor 12:17-18 (NIV)

By the time Paul speaks of Titus again, Titus and the anonymous brother evidently had arrived in Corinth. They are accused of exploiting the Corinthians in the name of Paul. Paul announces his forthcoming arrival and proclaims that he is not at all interested in the possessions of the Corinthians.

> Now I am ready to visit you for the third time, and I will not be a burden to you, because what I want is not your possessions but you. After all, children should not have to save up for their parents, but parents for their children.   2 Cor 12:14 (NIV)

> This third time I will really visit you: "Every matter must be established by the testimony of two or three witnesses." I gave you a warning as

> if I were with you a second time although I am absent now: On my
> return I will not spare those who sinned earlier or any of the others....
> 2 Cor 13:1-2

These two passages are often understood as if Paul were
announcing a third visit to Corinth. This is the view of the translators
of the NIV and NRSV. They translate: "This will be my third visit to
you" (NIV), and "This is the third time I am coming to you" (NRSV).
The Greek text, however, is open to both interpretations. My understanding is based on 1–2 Corinthians as a unit. In 1 Cor 16:5 Paul is
ready to leave. In 2 Cor 1:15-17 he reflects on a plan to visit the
Corinthians before he goes to Macedonia, and he must have told
the Corinthians about this plan because he apologizes for not fulfilling this plan. In 2 Cor 13:1 he announces his visit the third time. In
my opinion, the text says that it is the third time Paul is ready to visit
Corinth and that he will really come this time, and his expression in
2 Cor 13:2 "as if I were with you a second time although I am absent
now" is to be understood as a definite statement that he has been to
Corinth only once.[28]

As far as the text of 1–2 Corinthians is concerned there is no need
to assume that Paul visited the Corinthians more than twice. It is one
of the editorial goals of Paul to present his changing plans in the
right light, and this is the reason why he expressly includes his travel
plans in his authorized recension of the Corinthian correspondence.

Romans. In the letter to the Romans Paul basically tells Romans two
things concerning his travel plans: that he had planned to visit them
many times but had been hindered from coming so far, and that he
is planning a journey to Spain and wants to visit the Christian
congregation in Rome while passing through.

> . . . and I pray that now at last by God's will the way may be opened
> for me to come to you. . . . I do not want you to be unaware,
> brothers, that I planned many times to come to you (but have been
> prevented from doing so until now). . . . Rom 1:10,13 (NIV)

> This is why I have often been hindered from coming to you. But now
> that there is no more place for me to work in these regions, and since
> I have been longing for many years to see you, I plan to do so when
> I go to Spain. I hope to visit you while passing through and to have
> you assist me on my journey there, after I have enjoyed your com-
> pany for a while. Now, however, I am on my way to Jerusalem in the

service of the saints there. . . . So after I have completed this task and
have made sure that they have received this fruit, I will go to Spain
and visit you on the way. . . . so that by God's will I may come to you
with joy and together with you be refreshed.

Rom 15:22-25,28,32 (NIV)

These passages are not irrelevant for the understanding of Romans
even for a later audience. They reflect the relationship between Paul
and the Christian congregation in Rome. If we group Romans, 1–2
Corinthians, and Galatians as a unit this is the only passage that tells
the reader that Romans was written after 1–2 Corinthians.

This leaves us with only one passage in Romans that would not
be of great interest for the reader of the letters of Paul, the recommendation of Phoebe.

I commend to you our sister Phoebe, a servant of the church in
Cenchrea. I ask you to receive her in the Lord in a way worthy of the
saints and to give her any help she may need from you, for she has
been a great help to many people, including me.   Rom 16:1-2 (NIV)

Phoebe is not mentioned anywhere else in the letters of Paul.
Once she arrived at her destination and presented Paul's recommendation no one needed to read the message again. This is the only
passage I can find in Romans, 1–2 Corinthians, and Galatians containing the kind of information I would suspect a later editor to
delete before publishing. It sounds much more like a private letter—
like the long list of greetings following this passage in Romans 16.

Summary. The notes on Paul's travels and plans left in Romans and
1–2 Corinthians give the reader an idea where Paul was at the time
when he wrote. Actually, Paul's travel plans are a major cause of
disagreement and thus form an important topic of the Corinthian
correspondence. There is only one passage—the sending of
Phoebe—that might seem irrelevant to a later reader. It bears information pertinent only for a short period of time.

Criterion of Selection

Why did Paul select his letters to the Romans, 1–2 Corinthians, and
Galatians to be published in the same collection? What is the common topic?

To help us find the answer, let us look at another example from a
compatible letter collection. During the time when Cyprian was
bishop of Carthage (248/49–258) a problem arose among Christian

communities. Several people who had belonged to non-Catholic congregations and had been baptized there converted to the Catholic church. Was it necessary for them to be baptized a second time? Cyprian together with other bishops insisted on a second baptism. They unanimously passed a synodal resolution (ep 70) on the subject. Some time later the Mauritanian bishop Quintus asked Cyprian for his advice in this matter, and Cyprian added a copy of the resolution to his answering letter, ep 71. Later another Mauritanian colleague, bishop Jubaianus, had the same request. Cyprian answered him in ep 73 and adds ep 71 and ep 70. Next Stephanus of Rome asked for advice and he got ep 70.71.73 with Cyprian's answer (ep 72). Finally Pompeius, who at the time probably was bishop of Sabrata in Tripolis, wrote, and together with Cyprian's answer (ep 74) he received the respectable collection ep 73.72.71.70. Naturally all the letters in the collection share a common topic—the question of a second baptism. This was the only reason to present them in the same collection. The common topic constitutes the criterion of selection.

Now let us apply this observation to the letters of Paul. What do Romans, 1–2 Corinthians, and Galatians have in common? Where does Paul make a connection between the three addressees, the Galatians, the Corinthians, and the Romans? Do these letters share a common topic?

Let us first investigate how Paul connects the three addressees. He does not speak of the Romans outside of Romans. There is, however, one passage where Paul refers to the Corinthians outside of the Corinthian correspondence, and one passage where he mentions the Galatian churches outside of the letter to the Galatians. Both passages speak of the same topic.

> For Macedonia and Achaia were pleased to make a contribution for the poor among the saints in Jerusalem.   Rom 15:26 (NIV)

> Now about the collection for God's people: Do what I told the Galatian churches to do. On the first day of every week, each one of you should set aside a sum of money in keeping with his income, saving it up, so that when I come no collections will have to be made.
>   1 Cor 16:1-2 (NIV)

Corinth was the capital of the senatorial province of Achaia. Paul addresses 2 Corinthians (2 Cor 1:1) "To the church of God in Corinth, together with all the saints throughout Achaia . . . " Therefore the Corinthians are included when Paul reports that Achaia has made "a contribution for the poor among the saints in Jerusalem" (Rom 15:26).

In 1 Corinthians Paul remarks that the Galatian churches as well are willing to participate in the "collection for God's people" (1 Cor 16:1). Both relevant passages speak of the collection. Is the collection a topic all four letters share? This is pretty clear for Romans and 1 Corinthians from the passages cited above. But what about Galatians and 2 Corinthians?

> All they asked was that we should continue to remember the poor, the very thing I was eager to do.   Gal 2:10 (NIV)

> So we urged Titus, since he had earlier made a beginning, to bring also to completion this act of grace on your part.   2 Cor 8:6 (NIV)

The collection for the poor in Jerusalem is mentioned in Galatians at a crucial point. In the conflict between Paul and the Jerusalem apostles, Paul presents the collection as the only requirement he was asked to follow: "All they asked was that we should continue to remember the poor. . . ." (Gal 2:10). And he readily agrees. At the end of 1 Corinthians (16:2) Paul describes how the technical part of the collection should be handled among the Galatian and Corinthian congregations. In 2 Corinthians the "service to the saints" (2 Cor 9:1) is treated extensively (2 Corinthians 8–9). And its successful completion is mentioned in Romans (15:26).

Summary. The collection is obviously one of the topics these four letters have in common. It could constitute the criterion of selection—that is to say, Paul's reason to select these four letters could be closely related to his fundraising campaign "for the poor among the saints in Jerusalem" (Rom 15:26).

To sum up my argument: comparable evidence proves that something must hold the four Pauline letters together. I asked the text, how does Paul connect such diverse addresses as Rome, Corinth, and Galatia? The two relevant passages speak of a collection for the poor in Jerusalem. This is a clue. And indeed, the collection is a topic all four letters share.

The Literary Genre of Romans, 1–2 Corinthians, and Galatians

The Letter to the Romans

So far we have seen that if we look at Romans, 1–2 Corinthians, and Galatians as a literary unit, the whole letter collection has only one passage that sounds very much like a private letter (Romans 16). Most of the people mentioned there by name play no role in the rest of the text. The recommendation of Phoebe is pertinent only for a short time. The impression is that we are reading someone else's mail. The greetings do not interest a broader audience; they are written for very specific people at a very specific time at a very specific occasion. There is no further significance.

What do we make of this? This passage is obviously a private letter. Paul greets those people by name for whom he put the collection Romans, 1–2 Corinthians, and Galatians together. There are analogies to this. The term I will use for this kind of greeting is "cover note."

Romans 16 as a Cover Note. There are many examples of a cover note being sent together with copies to the addressee for whom those copies were made.

When bishop Cyprian of Carthage sent a copy of the records of a synodal meeting to his colleague, the Mauritanian bishop Quintus, he states in his cover note: "To let you know what most of the bishops and presbyter-colleagues decided on this topic when they came together, I enclose a copy of their resolution" (ep 71:1).

A cover note has two characteristic features. First, it is never addressed to the same place as the original. There is no use sending copies to someone who has the original. And, second, we would expect cover notes to mention the enclosed copies. It might not always be absolutely necessary to refer to the enclosed copy. If the cover note is written in another hand on the same sheet of paper as the copy, it would be evident to the reader of the original. For example, if I were to send someone photocopies of an article, I would not necessarily write on the first copied page: "Dear Charles, these are the copies you asked for." This is obvious. However, it is characteristic for cover notes to greet, and very often they do make some kind of reference to the copy. In Romans 16 such a reference is made.

> I, Tertius, the writer of this letter, greet you in the Lord.
> Rom 16:22 (NRSV)

It is clear that Tertius does not want to say that he is the author of Romans. The expression is open for two interpretations: either "I wrote what Paul dictated" or "I copied the letter for you." If Romans 16 is a cover note, the second interpretation applies.

Autographic subscriptions are one of the characteristic features of the letters of Paul. Paul, like practically all ancient letter writers who could afford a secretary, wrote the last passages of his letters—the greetings—in his own hand. Then he passed the pen to Tertius, who wrote one sentence: "I, Tertius, . . . greet you." Then Paul takes the pen again and writes: "Gaius, whose hospitality I and the whole church here enjoy, sends you his greetings," and finishes the letter. When Tertius writes his sentence, the reader of the original will immediately realize that this was the hand who copied the enclosed letter to the Romans (Romans 1–15). This way Paul would prove that this was an authorized copy of Romans, even if the cover note was on a separate sheet. What better way to prove the authenticity of an enclosed copy?

Address of Romans 16. This leaves us with a second question. If Romans 16 is a cover note, then it probably was not addressed to Rome. For whom was the copy made? If we are able to identify the addressee of Romans 16, chances are we have found the people for whom the whole letter collection Romans, 1–2 Corinthians, Galatians was made.

There are only few names occurring in Romans 16 as well as in other places of the collection. Aquila and Priscilla are greeted in Romans 16:3. So they were not with Paul when he wrote Romans 16. They were with the addressee of Romans 16. On the other hand Aquila and Priscilla were with Paul when he wrote 1 Corinthians 16, because they send their greetings to the Corinthians (1 Cor 16:19), and Paul was in Ephesus when he wrote 1 Corinthians 16. This clearly suggests that Aquila and Priscilla lived in Ephesus and therefore Romans 16 is addressed to Ephesus.

Another observation corroborates this assumption. At one point Paul makes a geographical remark in connection with one of the greeted persons, Epenetus:

> Greet my dear friend Epenetus, who was the first convert to Christ in the province of Asia.   Rom 16:5b (NIV)

He describes Epenetus as the "first convert to Christ in the province of Asia." Epenetus obviously is one of the addressees of Romans 16, he lives in the "province of Asia," and Ephesus is the capital of this province.

But if Romans 16 is a cover note added later to Romans 1–15, doesn't the original letter Romans 1–15 end very unmotivated and abruptly?

The God of peace be with all of you. Amen.	Rom 15:33 (NRSV)
The grace of our Lord Jesus be with you.	Rom 16:20b (NRSV)
The grace of the Lord Jesus be with you.	1 Cor 16:23 (NRSV)
The grace of the Lord Jesus Christ, the love of God, and the communion of the Holy Spirit be with all of you.	2 Cor 13:13 (NRSV)
May the grace of our Lord Jesus Christ be with your spirit, brothers and sisters. Amen.	Gal 6:18 (NRSV)

The end of Romans 1–15 does not cause any difficulty. Paul comes to a decisive end. His final wish of peace (Rom 15:33) is very much like the endings of 1 Corinthians, 2 Corinthians, and Galatians. On the contrary, because Romans 16 contains a final wish as well (Rom 16:20b) understanding Romans 16 as a cover note explains this observation harmoniously. Two final wishes in the same letter are more than unusual, to say the least.[29]

Summary. We have seen that four of the letters of Paul—Romans, 1 Corinthians, 2 Corinthians, and Galatians—form a literary unit. Paul himself produced an authorized recension of these letters and edited the letters for friends in Ephesus.

The Corinthian Correspondence

We now turn to the literary character of 1–2 Corinthians. As I mentioned earlier, the riddle of 2 Corinthians was the first exegetical problem I really grappled with. I developed a theory over the years that I shall present here. I see it as an attempt to put pieces of a puzzle together to form a picture. It is the special concern of any historical introduction to the letters of Seneca, Pliny, or bishop Cyprian to discern what might be part of the original letter mailed and how much editing is to be expected when the authors prepared the first edition. We face the same problem when we look at a modern letter collection like *Die Leiden des jungen Werthers* by Wolfgang Goethe. No doubt those letters cover detailed biographical events in the life of their authors. And still, if the authors chose to use material from more than one letter, they felt free to do so.

There are strong indications in 1–2 Corinthians that not all of the material used was written at the same time, especially the different situations referred to in the text and the sudden changes of attitude in 2 Corinthians. First Paul waits for Titus in Troas but does not meet him, then Paul meets Titus in Macedonia and sends him back to Corinth, and then Titus is in Corinth again. Other observations that might indicate later editing are the unexpected digressions so typical for 1–2 Corinthians.

On the other hand the missing letters Paul refers to are a drawback for any theory of a carefully prepared edition, because references to missing letters convey poor editing. Why did he not delete those references? I will attempt to show that it is not necessary to assume that the letters referred to in the Corinthian correspondence are lost.

Here are the pieces to our puzzle: Paul edited 1–2 Corinthians for his friends in Ephesus. He used the originals he had easy access to while he stayed in Corinth and arranged the material in two blocks. He does not refer to any missing letters.

Now let us see what picture emerges when we put the pieces together.

Two Blocks. I will deal with the most apparent question first. If Paul carefully edited the material he wrote to the Corinthians, why does he organize the text in two blocks? The canonical edition refers to these blocks as 1 Corinthians and 2 Corinthians. Bearing in mind that Paul addresses his work to his friends in Ephesus, the answer is easy. The point where 1 Corinthians ends and 2 Corinthians begins, is when Paul left Ephesus. Up to this point his friends in Ephesus were well informed about his relationship to the Corinthians. They knew the people who had visited Paul, so Paul left the names of those people in the text when he had the copy of the originals made. And his friends knew that Paul wrote more than a single letter to the Corinthians before he left Ephesus.

Criteria. The traditional view of 1–2 Corinthians is that they are two separate letters Paul wrote to the Christian congregation in Corinth. I will show, however, that 1–2 Corinthians were put together from several letters Paul wrote to the Corinthians. I will prove the point by looking at other ancient letters again. It is possible to describe a typical letter. And the analysis allows some judgment on determining where a letter begins or ends or which passages cannot be part of the same letter. For example, a new letter should have a fresh start. We would not expect a syntactical connection like "and," "or," or some such. We would expect a fresh introduction and new topics. References to topics of older letters would have to be more elaborate, noting, for example, that this or that was already covered in a previous letter.

There are formal elements such as greetings that usually occur at the beginning of a letter ("Dear . . .") or at the end of a letter ("With warmest regards"). Much research has been done on this. The data for ancient letters has been collected and grouped. When formal elements that usually occur at the end of a letter are followed by passages containing elements that usually occur at the beginning of letters, this can easily be interpreted as a sign that two letters were combined at this point. We have already discussed at length one kind of typical passage at the end of a dictated letter—the autographic subscription.[30]

Again, it is typical for a letter writer to tell the reader where he got new information; for example many letters start out with a note that the letter writer just received a letter from the addressee. And because letters in antiquity were usually delivered by personal messengers, very often these messengers are referred to in the letter. And because only one messenger per letter is needed, if the text refers to more than one messenger, it consists of more than one letter. And if the text gives more than one source of information, this suggests that it was put together from more than one letter.

Methodological Reflection. I shall attempt to show in the following interpretation that 1 Corinthians and 2 Corinthians contain material from several of Paul's letters, not just two. The letters are edited together in chronological order. Different messengers who delivered the letter or who brought new information that gave occasion for Paul to write further are usually mentioned. Elements typical of letter endings and beginnings are still discernable, thus enabling us today to determine where one letter ended and the next one started. Sometimes it is even clear that Paul was at different geographical locations when he wrote. Specifically, I will show that 1 Corinthians was put together from the material of three letters and 2 Corinthians from the material of four letters. So the original correspondence actually consisted of seven letters. It is not necessary to assume that any of the letters to the Corinthians which Paul refers to in 1–2 Corinthians are missing.

First Letter 1 Cor 1:10—4:21: "There Are Quarrels among You." The first messengers Paul mentions in 1 Corinthians are people of the household of Chloe. He cites them as his source of information. They had informed him of quarrels among the Corinthian congregation. Thus 1 Corinthians 1–4 deals with quarrels. Then at the end of this passage Paul mentions the second messenger—Timothy—whom he sends to the Corinthians.

> For it has been reported to me by Chloe's people that there are quarrels among you, my brothers and sisters.   1 Cor 1:11 (NRSV)

> I appeal to you, then, be imitators of me. For this reason I sent you Timothy, who is my beloved and faithful child in the Lord, to remind you of my ways in Christ Jesus, as I teach them everywhere in every church.   1 Cor 4:16-17 (NRSV)

It is likely that Paul sent Timothy back with the letter he had just finished. We see in these passages both the source of information that prompted Paul to write and the name and recommending comments that usually are written to authorize the messenger who brought Paul's written answer back to Corinth.

Second Letter 1 Cor 5:1—6:11: The Case of the Immoral Brother. By the next time Paul refers to new information, reports of sexual immorality had reached him. New information is an indication of a new letter. This time, however, he does not reveal his source.

> It is actually reported that there is sexual immorality among you, and of a kind that is not found even among pagans; for a man is living with his father's wife.   1 Cor 5:1 (NRSV)

Evidently Paul is referring to only one person in the congregation who is involved in a sexual affair of which Paul disapproves. Paul's advice is to expel the sinner.

> You are to hand this man over to Satan for the destruction of the flesh, so that his spirit may be saved in the day of the Lord.
>   1 Cor 5:5 (NRSV)

The following sentences (1 Cor 5:9-11) usually are understood as a reference to a missing letter. But this passage can just as well be understood as Paul's reflection on the letter he is currently writing.

> I wrote to you in my letter not to associate with sexually immoral persons—not at all meaning the immoral of this world, or the greedy and robbers, or idolaters, since you would then need to go out of the world. But now I am writing to you not to associate with anyone who bears the name of brother or sister who is sexually immoral or greedy, or is an idolater, reviler, drunkard, or robber. Do not even eat with such a one.   1 Cor 5:9-11 (NRSV)

Paul is clearly referring to the topic he was just writing about. Very often at the end of a letter we find a passage where the writer reflects on the letter he is just finishing. So, for example at the end of his letter to the Romans, Paul explains why he wrote "quite boldly on some points" (Rom 15:15) although he had never been to Rome and therefore did not know the congregation.

> I have written you quite boldly on some points, as if to remind you of them again, because of the grace God gave me. . . . Rom 15:15 (NIV)

Or at the end of the letter to the Hebrews and at the end of 1 Peter the authors excuse themselves for not having written a longer letter.

> Brothers, I urge you to bear with my word of exhortation, for I have written you only a short letter.   Heb 13:22 (NIV)

> With the help of Silas, whom I regard as a faithful brother, I have written to you briefly, encouraging you and testifying that this is the true grace of God. Stand fast in it.   1 Pet 5:12 (NIV)

Thus it is a rather common formal element at the end of a letter for a writer to reflect on what he had just written.[31] In 1 Cor 5:9-11 Paul reflects on what he had just written. He clearly refers to "sexually immoral people" and "not to associate with" them. And therefore it sounds very much like a passage taken from the end of a letter.

Paul does not give us the name of the man who had an affair with his "father's wife." But he refers to a very specific case. He does not discuss sexual immorality as such. He tells the congregation in detail what to do with this man. Paul knew the name of the man and I am sure that he recorded his name in the original letter. However, the name is of no special interest to the reader of the letter collection. The important information is how to deal with someone like that. Whether or not the man repented and changed his behavior, Paul considered it better not to pass on his name to future generations and therefore he erased the name of the man when he prepared his authorized recension of 1 Corinthians. This is a typical case of *damnatio memoriae.*

The next time Paul clearly refers to a new source of information he cites from a letter he received.

> Now for the matters you wrote about: It is good for a man not to marry.   1 Cor 7:1 (NIV)

Third Letter 1 Cor 6:12—16:24: Answering a Letter from Corinth. A new source of information is again a sign for a new letter. But it is obvious that Paul's letter did not start at this point, because the passage is syntactically connected to the preceding text. The NIV translates this connection with the phrase, "Now for the matters you wrote about . . ." The word "now" connects the passage to the preceding text. So what we have to look for in the preceding context is a fresh beginning.

1 Cor 6:12 looks very much like a new beginning. This would imply that the letter about the "Case of the Immoral Brother" contained another passage about "Lawsuits among Believers" and then came to an end. What makes 1 Cor 6:12 appear to be the beginning of a new letter is that Paul outlines several topics he will discuss in the following chapters.

> "Everything is permissible for me"—but not everything is beneficial. "Everything is permissible for me"—but I will not be mastered by anything.
>   "Food for the stomach and the stomach for food"—but God will destroy them both. The body is not meant for sexual immorality, but for the Lord, and the Lord for the body. By his power God raised the Lord from the dead, and he will raise us also.   1 Cor 6:12-14 (NIV)

"Everything is permissible for me—but not everything is beneficial" (1 Cor 6:12) is repeated word for word in 1 Cor 10:23. The context there is the question whether or not it was acceptable for a Christian to eat meat that had been sacrificed to idols. And food is exactly the topic of the following verse (1 Cor 6:13): " 'Food for the stomach and the stomach for food'—but God will destroy them both." "The body is not meant for sexual immorality, but for the Lord, and the Lord for the body" (1 Cor 6:13) relates easily to 1 Corinthians 7, where Paul proposes marriage as the Christian alternative to sexual immorality. Finally, "by his power God raised the Lord from the dead, and he will raise us also" refers to the essence of 1 Corinthians 15, where Paul discusses the resurrection of Christ.

After Paul gives the reader his source of information—a letter from Corinth—he introduces the first topic of this letter with a Greek phrase that can be translated, "Now about . . ." From this point on Paul uses exactly the same phrase several times when he introduces a new topic. A simple explanation for this is that Paul refers to the letter from the Corinthians each time he uses this phrase.

Now for the matters you wrote about: It is good for a man not to marry.   1 Cor 7:1 (NIV)

Now about virgins . . . .   1 Cor 7:25 (NIV)

Now about food sacrificed to idols . . . .   1 Cor 8:1 (NIV)

Now about spiritual gifts . . . .   1 Cor 12:1 (NIV)

Now about the collection for God's people . . . .   1 Cor 16:1 (NIV)

If this conclusion is correct then Paul is still answering the letter from Corinth in 1 Corinthians 16—the last chapter of 1 Corinthians. In this chapter Paul gives us the names of visitors from Corinth. And again it is not difficult to imagine that those men—Stephanas, Fortunatus, and Achaicus—were the ones who delivered to Paul the letter from Corinth.

I was glad when Stephanas, Fortunatus and Achaicus arrived, because they have supplied what was lacking from you.   1 Cor 16:17 (NIV)

And in the same chapter Paul asks the Corinthians to welcome Timothy, the messenger Paul had sent back to Corinth to deliver his reply (1 Cor 6:12—16:21).

If Timothy comes, see to it that he has nothing to fear while he is with you, for he is carrying on the work of the Lord, just as I am. No one, then, should refuse to accept him. Send him on his way in peace so that he may return to me. I am expecting him along with the brothers.
                                                                           1 Cor 16:10-11 (NIV)

My three major elements—that it is common for private letters to mention the source of new information, to name the messenger who brings the news, and to recommend the messenger who delivers the letter are not indisputable as regards this third letter. Reference to a letter from Corinth is not the only possible interpretation for Paul's repeated phrase "now about . . . ." The text does not expressly say that Stephanas and his colleagues delivered a letter from Corinth; they could just as well be those who brought Paul's answer back to Corinth. And as far as Timothy is concerned the text is open to interpretation that Paul expected Timothy to arrive in Corinth after his letter reached Corinth. There are more possible interpretations, thus multiplying the number of possible combinations.

Note Paul's expression that he expects Timothy back "along with the brothers" (1 Cor 16:11). This certainly is not the way to write a personal letter. I believe that the original definitely contained the names of the brothers. Paul deleted them because he did not think that they were of any interest for the audience of his letter collection—namely his friends in Ephesus.

2 Corinthians takes over where 1 Corinthians left off. There are three points in 2 Corinthians where the text begins fresh: 2:14, 7:4, and 10:1. Those are the places where one letter ends and the next one begins. Each letter can easily be related to a different situation in Paul's journey.[32]

Fourth Letter 2 Cor 1:3—2:11: A Letter of Grief. In 2 Cor 1:3—2:11 Paul talks about "the hardships we suffered in the province of Asia" (2 Cor 1:8). Reading 1–2 Corinthians as a unit the passage is placed between Paul's stay in Ephesus (1 Cor 16:8) and his departure from Troas to Macedonia (2 Cor 2:12-13).

The main topic of this part of 2 Corinthians is Paul's excuse for not visiting the Corinthians before he left for Macedonia. He makes it very clear that he feels unhappy about what is going on in Corinth and wants to spare himself a "painful visit."

> I planned to visit you on my way to Macedonia and to come back to you from Macedonia, and then to have you send me on my way to Judea. . . . I call God as my witness that it was in order to spare you that I did not return to Corinth. . . . So I made up my mind that I would not make another painful visit to you.
>
> 2 Cor 1:16,23; 2:1 (NIV)

Paul was evidently upset with the Corinthians when he wrote this letter. The following text usually is interpreted as a reference to a previous letter that Paul had sent to the Corinthians.

> For if I grieve you, who is left to make me glad but you whom I have grieved? I wrote as I did so that when I came I should not be

distressed by those who ought to make me rejoice. I had confidence in all of you, that you would all share my joy. For I wrote you out of great distress and anguish of heart and with many tears, not to grieve you but to let you know the depth of my love for you.

2 Cor 2:2-4 (NIV)

Then Paul refers to someone "who has caused grief" and asks the Corinthians "to forgive and comfort him" (2 Cor 2:5-8).

I wrote for this reason: to test you and to know whether you are obedient in everything.   2 Cor 2:9 (NRSV)

The literal translation of the Greek in 2 Cor 2:9 is: "Another reason I wrote you. . . ." This translation makes the connection to the first reason—the changed traveling plan (2 Cor 2:2)—clearer. Again it is not necessary to assume an older letter. Paul reflects on the letter he is just finishing. He talks about the grief he feels while writing and about his reasons for writing—exactly as he did at the end of Romans (Rom 15:15).

Let us visualize the picture again. At the end of his letters Paul would pick up the pen himself and add a subscription in his own hand. It is easy to imagine that this happened after his final word that he "would not make another painful visit." Literally the text reads: "So I made up my mind, not to come again to you in grief." It was very characteristic for autographic subscriptions to repeat an idea contained in the preceding text. Paul picks up the Greek word for "grief" in the preceding text and plays on it. He uses the word no less than seven times in the following sentences (2 Cor 2:2-8). And when he formulates "I wrote as I did . . ." or "Another reason I wrote you . . ." he uses exactly the same Greek expression for "I wrote" as he does at the beginning of the autographic subscription in Galatians.

See what large letters I make when I am writing in my own hand!

Gal 6:11 (NRSV)

This Greek expression for "I wrote" (aorist) is open to an English translation in the present tense as well; therefore, it is just as valid to translate 2 Cor 2:9, "Another reason I write to you is to find out if you stand the test and if you are obedient in everything." This meaning fits the context much better. It explains why Paul is so full of joy when he receives news later, that the Corinthians had stood the test and Titus could report to him about their "longing for" Paul, their "deep sorrow and ardent concern" for him, so Paul's "joy was greater than ever" (2 Cor 7:7).

Fifth Letter 2 Cor 2:14—7:3: "Must we commend ourselves again?"
Another sign that one letter ends and a new letter begins is the
expression of thanks to God with which 2 Cor 2:14—7:3 starts out.
As we have already seen, an expression of thanks is the most
characteristic formal element at the beginning of the letters of Paul.
With the exception of Galatians, Hebrews, 1 Timothy, and Titus, all
of the letters of the canonical edition of the letters of Paul start out
this way.

> But thanks be to God, who always leads us in triumphal procession in
> Christ and through us spreads everywhere the fragrance of the knowl-
> edge of him.   2 Cor 2:14 (NIV)

No connection exists between the preceding text and 2 Cor 2:14—
7:3; the travel plans are not mentioned and the punishment of the
sinner is not mentioned.

If the Corinthian correspondence is read as a unit, the situation in
2 Cor 2:14—7:3 is framed by Paul's departure from Troas to Macedonia (2 Cor 2:12-13) and his arrival in Macedonia (2 Cor 7:5). The
only messenger mentioned is Titus. Paul had hoped to meet him in
Troas with news from Corinth but had to leave for Macedonia before
Titus arrived. Paul arrives in Macedonia and feels discouraged and
depressed, or as Paul described it later in his own words: "For when
we came into Macedonia, this body of ours had no rest, but we were
harassed at every turn—conflicts on the outside, fears within" (2 Cor
7:5 NIV). Specifically he has no idea how the Corinthians would react
to his letter (2 Cor 1:3—2:11). This is the situation the context
assigns to 2 Cor 2:14—7:3.

In this light Paul's theologically profound explanation of his godly
ministry makes this letter sound very much like a letter of self-
recommendation. He is very aware of this and mentions it twice.

> Are we beginning to commend ourselves again? Or do we need, like
> some people, letters of recommendation to you or from you?
>   2 Cor 3:1 (NIV)

> We are not trying to commend ourselves to you again, but are giving
> you an opportunity to take pride in us. . . .   2 Cor 5:12 (NIV)

This fifth letter to the Corinthians is carefully designed to culmi-
nate in the final exclamation; everything is written to stress the last
point. Paul again reflects on the letter he is just finishing and gives
us his reason for writing. To cite Paul's own words (2 Cor 6:11-13;
7:2 NIV), "We have spoken freely to you, Corinthians, and opened

wide our hearts to you. We are not withholding our affection from you, but you are withholding yours from us. As a fair exchange—I speak as to my children—open wide your hearts also. . . . Make room for us in your hearts."

Sixth Letter 2 Cor 7:4—9:15: The Collection. In 2 Cor 7:4 a sudden change takes place. No self-recommendation on the side of Paul is necessary anymore. He has "great confidence" in the Corinthians, takes "great pride" in them; he feels "greatly encouraged" and "his joy knows no bounds." As I pointed out before, this sudden change of attitude is one of the most interesting features of 2 Corinthians and for the exegete probably the most challenging question to settle. How can this be explained? Once again, the sudden change marks the beginning of a new letter. And Paul explains the new situation in a very complete way by telling us where he was when he wrote 2 Cor 7:4—9:15. When he receives new information, he gives us the name of the messenger that came from the Corinthians and mentions the messengers he sent back with the letter and—as we would expect—he even reflects on the reason for writing the letter he is just writing.

But let us answer one question at a time. Where was the letter written? In Macedonia. When? Paul had stayed in Macedonia for an indefinite period of time before Titus, the messenger from Corinth, arrived and broke the good news. Paul sends Titus back to Corinth accompanied by several well-known brothers. His mission is to deliver a letter about the "service to the saints" (2 Cor 9:1) and together with the brothers "to finish the arrangements for the generous gift" (2 Cor 9:5) they had promised. Paul refers to a letter he had previously written.

> Even if I caused you sorrow by my letter, I do not regret it. . . . So even though I wrote to you, it was not on account of the one who did the wrong or of the injured party, but rather that before God you could see for yourselves how devoted to us you are.   2 Cor 7:8a.12 (NIV)

"Even if I caused you sorrow by my letter, I do not regret it" (2 Cor 7:8a). This is the third passage that has given rise to speculations about lost letters of the Corinthian correspondence. Others interpret the passage as a reference to 1 Corinthians. But is the character of 1 Corinthians correctly described with the words "I caused you sorrow"? Hardly.

Recall that in his subscription in the "Letter of Grief," Paul wrote about the grief he felt when he wrote the letter (2 Cor 2:2-4) and about someone who did something wrong (2 Cor 2:5-8). Both topics are mentioned as part of the letter Paul is talking about here. The word for "sorrow" is the word for "grief" Paul used so abundantly. He uses it again here, repeating it eight times (2 Cor 7:8-11). And the other topic he refers to he calls "the man who did the wrong." Obviously, Paul is talking about his "Letter of Grief" (2 Cor 1:3—2:11).

Now about the subscription. Where did the autographic subscription start? I think it begins with 2 Cor 9:1.

> There is no need for me to write to you about this service to the saints. For I know your eagerness to help. . . .   2 Cor 9:1-2a (NIV)

Paul begins again by reflecting on the letter he is just finishing: "There is no need for me to write to you about this service to the saints." He clearly picks up the topic of the preceding text. Despite what he says, there is a need for Paul to write. This need is urgent, and it is confidential. Confidential notes are characteristic in autographic subscriptions.

> For I know your eagerness to help, and I have been boasting about it to the Macedonians, telling them that since last year you in Achaia were ready to give; and your enthusiasm has stirred most of them to action. But I am sending the brothers in order that our boasting about you in this matter should not prove hollow, but that you may be ready, as I said you would be. For if any Macedonians come with me and find you unprepared, we—not to say anything about you—would be ashamed of having been so confident. So I thought it necessary to urge the brothers to visit you in advance and finish the arrangements for the generous gift you had promised. Then it will be ready as a generous gift, not as one grudgingly given.   2 Cor 9:2-5 (NIV)

Paul vividly describes the difficult situation he got himself into. To motivate the Macedonians to participate generously in his fundraising campaign for the saints in Jerusalem, Paul had boasted that the Corinthians were enthusiastic about it and he writes, "your enthusiasm has stirred most of them to action" (2 Cor 9:2). He should have known better. When Titus arrived and described the situation pertaining to the collection in Corinth, Paul must have realized how bad it was. What would happen if the poorer Macedonian congregations who had managed to raise a considerable sum would accompany him and then find out that the Corinthians had not even begun to collect? Would he not lose face? Would this not make him look like a liar? However, this was the reason he sent the delegation, entrusting them with an official letter to encourage them to proceed with the collection, and a handwritten subscription at the end, a secret and confidential message that had to be concealed from the Macedonians.

Seventh Letter 2 Cor 10:1—13:14: "I am not inferior to those super-apostles!" 2 Corinthians 10 is a fresh start. No direct connections to the preceding text can be detected. Paul does not tell us his source of information, but he did have news from Corinth. Bad news. It is somehow related to the letters he had written to the Corinthians.

> I do not want to seem to be trying to frighten you with my letters. For some say, "His letters are weighty and forceful, but in person he is unimpressive and his speaking amounts to nothing."
>
> 2 Cor 10:9-10 (NIV)

This is the fourth passage that was often interpreted as proof of lost letters of the Corinthian correspondence. Because if Paul only wrote one letter (1 Corinthians) before he wrote 2 Corinthians, how can he speak about "my letters" in the plural? But this fits my theory very well because the passage is taken from the seventh and last letter Paul wrote to the Corinthians.

Paul does not inform the reader about his source of information. But he does tell us that he is writing after Titus and the ominous brother he had sent had arrived at Corinth.

> Did I exploit you through any of the men I sent you? I urged Titus to go to you and I sent our brother with him. Titus did not exploit you, did he? Did we not act in the same spirit and follow the same course?
>
> 2 Cor 12:17-18 (NIV)

The delegation that accompanied Titus had a mission to collect money. And that was the problem—money: "Titus did not exploit you, did he?" (2 Cor 12:18) and "Now I am ready to visit you for the third time, and I will not be a burden to you, because what I want is not your possessions but you" (2 Cor 12:14).

With this we have reached the end of the Corinthian correspondence.

Redactional Notes Added. Some of the unexpected digressions of the Corinthian correspondence look very much like notes Paul added when he put the Corinthian material together, for example, the "Hymn of Love" (1 Corinthians 13). I will interpret 1 Corinthians 9 as a redactional note later, but I will not deal with all of the pertinent passages. The frame of the composition (1 Cor 1:1-3; 2 Cor 2:1-2, and 2 Cor 13:11-14) was probably not part of the original private correspondence. And 2 Cor 2:12-13, which tells that Paul left Troas for Macedonia, was probably added later by Paul to inform the Ephesians where one letter ends and the next one begins.

Interpreting the Names of 1 Corinthians. Although we have talked about them before, I want to add another comment on the many personal names in 1 Corinthians. As we have seen, 1 Corinthians contains more names than the letter to the Galatians, 2 Corinthians, or Romans, with the exception of Romans 16. 1 Corinthians 16 was written in Ephesus and the congregation in Ephesus must have at least met the Corinthian delegation of Fortunatus, Achaicus, and Stephanas who informed Paul; they probably met the delegation of Chloe as well. Paul left the names in the text because the Ephesians were familiar with them.

Both times when Paul refers to Aquila and Priscilla he mentions that "the church . . . meets at their house" (1 Cor 16:19; Rom 16:4-5). They most certainly were prominent members of the Ephesian congregation and there was no reason to remove their names.

Paul sends greetings to the Ephesians from a man named Gaius in Rom 16:23: "Gaius, whose hospitality I and the whole church here enjoy, sends you his greetings." Obviously the Ephesians knew him. And if this is the same man Paul is talking about in 1 Corinthians that might be another reason why Paul did not delete Gaius's name in 1 Cor 1:14: "I am thankful that I did not baptize any of you except Crispus and Gaius."

The Letter to the Galatians

Now let us investigate the literary genre of the letter to the Galatians. We have already noted that Galatians has no greetings at all. There are no traveling plans mentioned, there are no fellow workers sent. It is not even clear to whom Paul is writing. The term Galatia is not precise at all. Up to this day New Testament scholars cannot settle the question of the precise address. Galatia is either a geographical region or the Roman province. In both cases it covers a huge area. None of Paul's other letters has a comparable address.

Another interesting observation is related to the autographic subscription of Galatians (6:11-18). It resembles the kind of subscription found in legal documents. It is neither a confidential note, nor does it add anything new; it picks up a main topic from the body of the letter—a polemic against a certain group who tried to compel the Galatians to be circumcised. Central topics of Galatians referred to in the autographic subscription are circumcision, obeying the law, and the relevance of the cross.

> It is those who want to make a good showing in the flesh that try to compel you to be circumcised—only that they may not be persecuted for the cross of Christ. Even the circumcised do not themselves obey the law, but they want you to be circumcised so that they may boast about your flesh. May I never boast of anything except the cross of our Lord Jesus Christ, by which the world has been crucified to me, and I to the world.   Gal 6:12-14 (NRSV)

> But my friends, why am I still being persecuted if I am still preaching circumcision? In that case the offense of the cross has been removed.
>   Gal 5:11 (NRSV)

> And those who belong to Christ Jesus have crucified the flesh with its passions and desires.   Gal 5:24 (NRSV)

Summary. Galatians is completely lacking the formal elements of a private letter. If it is not a private letter, what else could it be? The autographic subscription has been analyzed and found to be very much like the authorization in legal documents. Galatians has the literary character of an authorized document.

The Intention of Paul's Letter Collection

Criterion of Selection:
Collection for Jerusalem

I have already demonstrated that one of the themes that hold the four canonical letters together is Paul's fundraising campaign for the poor in Jerusalem. But the collection as such does not play the central role we would expect it to play if it formed the criterion of selection for the collection. But it may be related to something else, something very important to Paul.

Using the collection as a clue, I will look for other topics related to Paul's fundraising. Why did he combine those four letters?

Key to Interpretation:
Reversed Chronology

There are two good rules when looking for the intention of an editor. First, we should begin with an analysis of those texts that are the closest in time to the editor. Second, the editorial intention very often is expressed clearly at the beginning or at the end of a text. These passages are very apt to contain editorial changes.

Now that we have established a relative chronology for the four letters, we can see that the last text to be written was the cover note to the Ephesians (Romans 16), followed by the letter to the Romans (Romans 1–15), which was probably written at the same time as the letter to the Galatians received its final form. The next oldest text would be the redactional parts of 1–2 Corinthians, followed by the passages of the original correspondence preserved in 2 Corinthians; the oldest material would be what is left of Paul's original letters to Corinth in 1 Corinthians.

Romans 16

Let us begin with the cover note to the Ephesians (Romans 16). Most of the text addresses specific individuals; Paul calls them by name, and they all seem to be his friends. But there is one passage that contains a warning of some unnamed people who "cause divisions," "contrary to the teaching you have learned" (Rom 16:17-18). No details are given.

> I urge you, brothers, to watch out for those who cause divisions and put obstacles in your way that are contrary to the teaching you have learned. Keep away from them. For such people are not serving our Lord Christ, but their own appetites. By smooth talk and flattery they deceive the minds of naive people. Everyone has heard about your obedience, so I am full of joy over you; but I want you to be wise about what is good, and innocent about what is evil.
>
> Rom 16:17-19 (NIV)

Who are "those who cause divisions"? Paul's defamation that such "people are not serving our Lord Christ" conveys almost beyond doubt that those people considered themselves true Christians.

Romans 1–15

Let us turn to the next oldest text, the letter to the Romans (Romans 1–15). The very last sentence before the final blessing mentions people Paul is so afraid of that he asks his Roman readers to pray that he might be rescued from them.

> I appeal to you, brothers and sisters, by our Lord Jesus Christ and by the love of the Spirit, to join me in earnest prayer to God on my behalf, that I may be rescued from the unbelievers in Judea, and that my ministry to Jerusalem may be acceptable to the saints, so that by God's will I may come to you with joy and be refreshed in your company. Rom 15:30-32 (NRSV)

Paul is afraid of "unbelievers in Judea." The Greek word literally means "disobedient people." Paul uses the term four more times in his letter to the Romans to describe non-Christians (2:8; 10:21; 11:30,31). But Paul is not only concerned about some unspecified non-Christian group in Judea, he is not even sure if his Christian brothers and sisters in Jerusalem are willing to accept his ministry; that is, he does not know if they will take the money that Paul raised in Galatia, Macedonia, and Achaia.

Here we have another clue—there is a close connection between the collection and the "saints in Jerusalem." Paul is not sure if the money will be acceptable to them. Remember that the people Paul warned the Ephesians about in his cover note (Rom 16:17-19) considered themselves to be Christians! Is Paul talking about the same persons in both places? Are "those who cause divisions" (Rom 16:17) to be identified as saints in Jerusalem?

The whole story takes on a macabre tone. Suddenly it sounds more like a story of money and crime than a passage from the New Testament. But what in the world has happened that causes Paul to feel so insecure?

Galatians

Let us have Paul explain the events to us in his own words. Of all the letters of Paul, the letter to the Galatians is his most elaborate and most carefully structured writing. Recent research has shown that the structure of Galatians fits with complete perfection the rhetorical rules laid out in the handbooks of the time.[33] Galatians is not a casual private letter; this is a carefully prepared text, structured to the smallest detail and authorized by a personal subscription.

Let us first note that our two clues—the "saints in Jerusalem" and the "collection for the poor"—are a major topic of Galatians. The passage where Paul mentions the collection is his promise (Gal 2:10) "to remember the poor." This is closely tied to negotiations with Christians in Jerusalem. The central topic, however, is different—it is his ministry.

We did not give in to them for a moment, so that the truth of the gospel might remain with you. As for those who seemed to be important—whatever they were makes no difference to me; God does not judge by external appearance—those men added nothing to my message. On the contrary, they saw that I had been entrusted with the task of preaching the gospel to the Gentiles, just as Peter had been to the Jews. For God, who was at work in the ministry of Peter as an apostle to the Jews, was also at work in my ministry as an apostle to the Gentiles. James, Peter, and John, those reputed to be pillars, gave me and Barnabas the right hand of fellowship when they recognized the grace given to me. They agreed that we should go to the Gentiles, and they to the Jews. All they asked was that we should continue to remember the poor, the very thing I was eager to do.

Gal 2:5-10 (NIV)

Paul's Adversaries. Let us reflect on the names again. As we have seen, Paul does not give any names of Galatian cities or Galatian Christians anywhere in his letter to the Galatians. But he does give the names of the apostles Peter, James, and John. And these names do not have a positive connotation. Paul is not terribly impressed by those men "who seemed to be important," "James, Peter, and John, those reputed to be pillars," "whatever they were makes no difference to me" and they "added nothing to my message."

What do we make of this? If we understand the first four letters of Paul as a literary unit that he put together and edited for his friends in Ephesus, this is the place where Paul identifies the Christian adversaries he was talking about in his cover letter to the collection (Romans 16). Although Paul's letter is addressed to the Galatians, in Paul's eyes the reason for the conflict originated somewhere else— in Jerusalem. Paul bases his defense on the fact that at some time the Jerusalem authorities—James, Peter, and John—had officially given him "the right hand of fellowship when they recognized the grace given to me" (Gal 2:9). He charges the saints in Jerusalem with breaking an old agreement.

But what exactly are they quarreling about? Paul's version states that the parties disagreed on his "ministry as an apostle to the Gentiles" (Gal 2:8). Although the Jerusalem authorities were skeptical in the beginning, they finally gave Paul their blessing for his work. But what part of his ministry was so difficult to accept? Following the quoted passage, Paul reports an incident in Antioch where he "opposed" Peter "to his face, because he was clearly in the wrong."

> When Peter came to Antioch, I opposed him to his face, because he
> was clearly in the wrong. Before certain people[34] came from James,
> he used to eat with the Gentiles. But when they arrived, he began to
> draw back and separate himself from the Gentiles because he was
> afraid of those who belonged to the circumcision group. The other
> Jews joined him in his hypocrisy, so that by their hypocrisy even
> Barnabas was led astray.   Gal 2:11-13 (NIV)

Paul accuses a group he calls the "circumcision group" of being
troublemakers. This term clearly carries a negative connotation. He
establishes a connection between this group, James, and Peter.
He accuses Peter of "hypocrisy."

Circumcision. Now we are beginning to get some color in the
picture. Circumcision is a major point of disagreement. Paul uses it
as an argument that "not even Titus, who was with me, was com-
pelled to be circumcised, even though he was a Greek" (Gal 2:3)
when Paul visited the Jerusalem authorities. Circumcision is treated
extensively in Galatians. For Paul it is completely out of the question
that it is not necessary to be circumcised to be a Christian. He is
aware that it was easier for Christians to communicate with the
Jewish community if they were circumcised. This way they could
present Christianity as a movement within the Jewish religion. But
Paul disagrees completely with this practice.

> But my friends, why am I still being persecuted if I am still preaching
> circumcision? In that case the offense of the cross has been removed.
>   Gal 5:11 (NRSV)

Christian Identity. Related to the topic of circumcision are other
problems as well concerning the Jewish law, like eating habits.
Eating with Gentiles actually provoked the incident in Antioch that
Paul is explaining to his readers in Galatians 2. For in those days it
was not yet clear that Christianity would form a religion of its own.
Jesus and his brother James, the twelve disciples and Paul, were all
Jews. From the perspective of Jews in Jerusalem, Christianity was just
another Jewish sect. Not so in Paul's eyes. No doubt, most of Paul's
letter to the Romans is written to describe his attitude toward his
Jewish brothers and sisters, and for the first time in literary history a
Christian theologian defines what it means to be a Christian in
contrast to being a Jew.

Money. There is another major point of disagreement between the Jerusalem authorities and Paul. It concerns the financing of their ministry.[35] Whereas in the Gospels Jesus insisted "Do not take along any gold or silver or copper in your belts . . . for the worker is worth his keep" (Matt 10:9-10) Paul proudly declares,

> I robbed other churches by receiving support from them so as to serve you. And when I was with you and needed something, I was not a burden to anyone, for the brothers who came from Macedonia supplied what I needed. I have kept myself from being a burden to you in any way, and will continue to do so.   (2 Cor 11:8-9 NIV)

The conflict is serious. Paul does not live up to the standard Jesus proclaimed. And even worse, Paul knows very well that he is not in accordance with what Jesus commanded; he knows that "the Lord has commanded that those who preach the gospel should receive their living from the gospel" (1 Cor 9:14).

> If others have this right of support from you, shouldn't we have it all the more? But we did not use this right. On the contrary, we put up with anything rather than hinder the gospel of Christ. Don't you know that those who work in the temple get their food from the temple, and those who serve at the altar share in what is offered on the altar? In the same way, the Lord has commanded that those who preach the gospel should receive their living from the gospel. But I have not used any of these rights.   1 Cor 9:12-15a (NIV)

Paul interprets the concept of Jesus not as a command but as a privilege, a privilege he does not need to take advantage of.[36]

Paul laments, "For if someone comes to you and preaches a Jesus other than the Jesus we preached, . . . or a different gospel from the one you accepted, you put up with it easily enough. But I do not think I am in the least inferior to those 'super-apostles' " (2 Cor 11:4-5). But is it not just the other way around? Is not the gospel the super-apostles preach—that is to say the apostles John and Peter, who had lived with Jesus for years, and James, the brother of Jesus who grew up with him—is not their version more authoritative, more convincing than Paul's? Is it not Paul who preaches a different gospel?

There is another aspect to the conflict, an aspect of quality. If someone tells you that you do not earn your money in an honest way, you would not easily put up with it, especially if you are working hard, and if you are as sure as Paul that you are fulfilling the ministry that God wants you to do. Although church history proves over and over again that Paul's concept of financing a mission is more practical and easier to manage than the concept of Jesus, Christian missionaries have not been able to settle the question to this day.

I was born in Africa as the son of missionaries. For my father and mother financing their ministry and their five children was not an academic dispute. My parents tried both methods; they accepted money from those who invited them to talk (Jesus' concept), they wrote books that sold very successfully, and for many years they even received a fixed salary from a mission board (Paul's concept). But I do not think that they ever had the feeling that they were working for money. Most of the time their ministry defined their schedule, and most of their work, such as counseling and letter writing, consisted of services no one paid them to perform. Perhaps this is the reason Paul reacts in such an aggressive way. He feels hurt. He feels misunderstood. He knows that he is fulfilling God's will.

For Paul marriage is a concession to those who "cannot control themselves" (1 Cor 7:9), a privilege no Christian needs to take advantage of, and he feels it more desirable to denounce this right. One of the very few times Paul refers expressly to Peter and very probably to James, the Lord's brother, outside of his letter to the Galatians, he talks about their marriages.

> Now to the unmarried and the widows I say: It is good for them to stay unmarried, as I am. But if they cannot control themselves, they should marry, for it is better to marry than to burn with passion.
> 1 Cor 7:8-9 (NIV)

> This is my defense to those who sit in judgment on me. Don't we have the right to food and drink? Don't we have the right to take a believing wife along with us, as do the other apostles and the Lord's brothers and Cephas [=Peter]? Or is it only I and Barnabas who must work for a living? 1 Cor 9:3-6 (NIV)

Now if we relate those two passages from 1 Corinthians 7 and 1 Corinthians 9 and keep in mind that he is addressing his opponents, it seems that Paul regards James and Peter as those kinds of Christians who cannot "control themselves." Paul surely was not trying to make a compliment with his subtle remark on the apostles' wives; and he becomes very, very personal. Remember Paul's defamation that the "circumcision group" preaches circumcision in order to avoid persecution (Gal 5:11), and that Paul refers to his adversaries as people "trying to pervert the gospel of Christ" (Gal 1:7). It does not require much of an imagination to realize how terribly unfair Paul is toward Peter and James.

Summary

Reading Romans, 1–2 Corinthians, and Galatians as a literary unit that was edited by Paul for friends in Ephesus provides the interpreter with information she or he will not get if the letters are treated separately. Not the many different situations of the original letters but the particular place and time when Paul produced the collection becomes important and serves as a guide to interpret the older material. This way of reading the texts allows us to fill in information lacking from one letter from the text of another letter and still feel comfortable that this was the way Paul wanted his friends to read this piece of literature. And suddenly the text reveals a story. The story of a conflict.

In the letter to the Romans Paul puts down his theological testament in a very abstract, general, and philosophical way. He covers positions that are in dispute between him and the Jerusalem authorities: the observance of the law, circumcision, and eating habits. He does not hesitate to inform the Romans about his fears, finishing the letter with a plea to pray for him (Rom 15:31) "that I may be rescued from the unbelievers in Judea and that my service in Jerusalem may be acceptable to the saints there."

I hold the letter to the Galatians to have the literary form of an authorized document, like an affidavit. It should be used by friends to prove his case against the saints in Jerusalem.

Corinth is one of the places where the conflict escalates. The first four chapters of 1 Corinthians deal with quarrels that originated around Peter and Paul. The last four chapters of 2 Corinthians reveal a culmination of this conflict.

The Ephesians knew that 1 Corinthians was composed of more than one letter, and they expected as much for 2 Corinthians as well. Paul gives them all the information he deems necessary for his friends in Ephesus to understand the setting.

Paul's request to support the collection brings up the old subject again. He had been faced before with the accusation of not being a good steward as far as money is concerned, because he clearly does not live up to Jesus' concept of financing a mission. And now Paul boldly asks the Galatians, the Macedonians, and the Corinthians for money. He asks for a collection that the saints in Jerusalem very evidently are not willing to accept from his hands.

The letter collection Romans, 1–2 Corinthians, Galatians is Paul's literary contribution to this conflict. In case of death it was designed to serve as his literary testament.

A Fictive Cover Note to Paul's Letter Collection

Paul, an apostle of Christ Jesus by the will of God. To the saints in Ephesus, the faithful in Christ Jesus. Grace and peace to you from God our Father and the Lord Jesus Christ.

Everyone has heard about your obedience, so I am full of joy over you. I urge you, brothers, by our Lord Jesus Christ and by the love of the Spirit, to join me in my struggle by praying to God for me. My body has no rest, I am harassed at every turn, I experience conflicts on the outside and fears within. Nevertheless, I am confident that the God of peace will soon crush Satan under our feet.

I have stayed in Corinth for several months now and had some of my letters copied for you. Because I am not sure if I will have time enough to visit you on my trip to Jerusalem, I prepare this cover note to explain the copies that will be forwarded to you in my name. If I shall not be able to see you in person, my messenger will inform you about what has happened to me.

As far as my correspondence with the church of God in Corinth and Achaia is concerned, I easily had access to the originals and the benefit of a secretary, Tertius, while I stayed in Corinth. Under my supervision Tertius copied the essence of the first three letters I sent to Corinth during my stay with you in Ephesus. I hope you will enjoy the comments, remarks, and explanations I asked Tertius to add at different places. I did not hold it necessary to mark where one letter ends and another one begins, because you were with me when I wrote them. However, I left the names of the various messengers from Corinth so you might remember the different situations. Feel free to show the letter composition to anyone who is interested in it. It will remind you of my way of life in Christ Jesus, which agrees with what I teach everywhere in every church, and I hope it will help you master the conflict you and the churches in Galatia are confronted with right now.

Furthermore, for your information, I send you copies of my correspondence with Corinth after I left Ephesus, all in all four more letters. The first of these letters I wrote in Troas shortly before I left for Macedonia. I added a note at the end of this letter so you can easily discern where the next letter starts. The other three letters I wrote in

Macedonia, one soon after our arrival, the next one after Titus had joined us and brought us good news from Corinth, the last one after Titus had travelled back to Corinth and the conflict with the "super-apostles" escalated. Tertius made a reliable copy from the originals—including my handwritten postscripts—but I asked him to leave out the names, greetings, and trivial passages to save time and paper and because they are neither of interest to you nor do they help promote my case.

As far as the trouble in Galatia is concerned, I do not see any reason to hide myself. I put down an affidavit of what actually happened and the essence of my message. You may show it to anyone who passes through Ephesus. There is no special address to send it to. Use it in the conflict to plead my case. There are so many lies put into the world by some who preach Christ out of selfish ambition, envy, and rivalry, I can easily imagine that someone might try to forge a letter in my name. Please take good care of the original and do not give it away. I addressed the affidavit to the churches in Galatia and authorized it with a subscription written in my own hand. So anyone who visits you and sees the original will know that it is authentic. Have copies made and hand them to trustworthy and obedient brothers who pass through Ephesus and travel to Galatia.

But my real enemies, those dogs, those men who do evil, those mutilators of the flesh, sit in Jerusalem. In a short time I will be able to talk to them directly and I will not spare them; they are demanding proof that Christ is speaking through me. I look forward to finding out not only how these arrogant people are talking, but what power they have. For the kingdom of God is not a matter of talk but of power. For the moment I cannot address them directly. That is the reason why I wrote an elaborate letter to the saints in Rome instead of a short note announcing my plans to visit them. (I would have had ample opportunity to send that kind of note from Judea.) In my letter I discuss a number of major points of disagreement with the false brothers in Jerusalem, especially concerning the right observance of the law. And I felt free to share my fears with the saints in Rome and asked them to pray for me, that I may be rescued from the disobedient brothers in Judea and survive my stay in Jerusalem. I am sure my adversaries in Jerusalem had a copy of the letter in their hands even before it reached Rome.

Brothers, I urge you to bear with my word of exhortation, for I have written you only a short letter. Greet all God's people. Grace be with you all.[37]

5
Postscript

We started out with the oldest existing manuscripts, looked at characteristic features of the letters of Paul, and interpreted them in the light of comparable ancient letter collections. Finally, we tried to understand the first four letters of our biblical edition of the letters of Paul as a collection that Paul himself had put together and prepared for publication.

Reading these four letters—the letter to the Romans, the two letters to the Corinthians, and the letter to the Galatians—as a literary unit made us aware of severe quarrels between the apostle Paul and the saints in Jerusalem with their leaders Peter and James. The first four letters of Paul present Paul's argument. They are radical. There is not much hope for peace to be found in them.

It is this conflict between Paul and the Jerusalem authorities that pushed Paul to publish four of his letters. And it is this conflict that later editors may have had in mind when they prepared a collection of Christian writings for publication, a collection that came to be known as the New Testament. Besides the fourteen letters of Paul we find letters of the Jerusalem authorities James, John, and Peter. (The author of 2 Peter makes it very clear that the apostle Peter is in complete agreement with Paul and writes in his letter, "just as our dear brother Paul also wrote you with the wisdom that God gave him"; 2 Pet 3:15, NIV.) We also find the four Gospels, which tell the story of Jesus from a Jerusalem perspective. Finally, we find the book of Acts, which combines the two authorities, the first half concentrating on the saints in Jerusalem and the second half on the life and mission of Paul. The picture conveyed by the writings of the

New Testament to their readers is one of unity. The conflict between Paul and Jerusalem was resolved.

Based on observations made with other ancient letter collections, I interpreted the first four letters of Paul as a literary unit. This is the major difference from other interpretations.

See what large letters I make when I am writing in my own hand! I believe that if we learn to read not only the letters of Paul, but also the whole New Testament as a literary unity we will read it as it was intended to be read by its first publishers. The text will provide us with a whole set of new insights, insights we miss as long as we treat each writing separately.
The grace of our Lord Jesus Christ be with you.

David Trobisch

Notes

1. The page is reproduced from *The Greek New Testament*, ed. K. Aland, M. Black, C. M. Martini, B. M. Metzger, and A. Wikgren (Stuttgart: Württemberg Bibelanstalt, 1966).

2. The reproduction is taken from Kurt and Barbara Aland, *The Text of the New Testament*, 2d ed. (Grand Rapids: Eerdmans, 1989).

3. Ibid., 91.

4. The reproduction is taken from Bruce M. Metzger, *Manuscripts of the Greek Bible: An Introduction to Greek Palaeography* (New York and Oxford: Oxford University Press, 1981), 105 (plate 28).

5. David Trobisch, *Die Entstehung der Paulusbriefsammlung: Studien zu den Anfängen christlicher Publizistik* (NTOA 10; Freiburg/Schweiz: Universitätsverlag; Göttingen: Vandenhoeck & Ruprecht, 1989).

6. The page of Codex Sinaiticus (ℵ01) is in a condition that makes it difficult to produce a good photograph. To demonstrate the evidence, the photo of the page containing Gal 5:20—Eph 1:9 given in H. J. Vogels, *Codicum Novi Testamenti Specimina* (Bonn: Haustein, 1929, 4) was scanned and then retouched with the help of a computer.

7. Gordon J. Bahr, "The Subscriptions in the Pauline Letters," *JBL* 87 (1968), 27–41. The quotation is taken from pp. 30–31.

8. *The Oxyrhynchus Papyri*, ed. Bernhard P. Grenfell, Arthur S. Hunt, part II (London, 1899), No. 246, 195–97, plate 7.

9. The English translation is taken from *Select Papyri in Four Volumes: I, Non-literary Papyri, Private Affairs*, with an English translation by A. S. Hunt and C. C. Edgar (The Loeb Classical Library; Cambridge, Mass., and London, 1970), 118, p. 315.

10. Between Phil 3:1 and Phil 3:2 Paul's tone shifts abruptly from joy and exhortation to aggressive warnings and furious insults (Phil 3:2): "Watch out for those dogs, those men who do evil, those mutilators of the flesh." But Paul's friendly attitude toward the addressee does not change; he argues

against a third party. Therefore it is not a parallel to Paul's changing attitude toward the recipients of the letter in 2 Corinthians.

11. To produce this text example I had to change the wording of the translation (NIV) slightly in order to show that the expression "as in all the congregations of the saints" could just as well form the final phrase of the preceding sentence. The Greek text definitely is open to this interpretation. This phrase does not necessarily introduce the following passage as most modern translations suggest.

12. A famous example of a passage that did not belong to the original text is John 7:53—8:11, the story about Jesus and the Adulterous Woman (John 8:7), "If anyone is without sin, let him be the first to throw a stone at her." This passage is missing in Codex Sinaiticus (‭א‬ 01) and Codex Vaticanus (B 03), the two oldest extant manuscripts of the Bible in Greek. The relevant pages of Codex Alexandrinus (A 02) and Codex Ephraemi Rescriptus (C 04) are not preserved anymore, but calculations based on the surrounding text show that these manuscripts did not contain the passage either. The passage was added later. The Authorized Byzantine Version presents the text following John 7:52, but four other places are extant in manuscripts as well: following John 7:36, John 21:25, Luke 21:38, and following Luke 24:53. The three manuscripts that render 1 Cor 14:34-35 following 1 Cor 14:40, i.e. the codices Claromontanus (D 06), Augiensis (F 010), and Boernerianus (G 012), provide nice examples for moving text to make the passage more readable in Romans 16. Rom 16:20b was moved after Rom 16:24, Rom 16:5a is moved behind Rom 16:3, and Rom 16:16b behind Rom 16:21, improving the style each time.

13. The reproduction and the transcription are taken from *The Chester Beatty Biblical Papyri: Descriptions and Texts of Twelve Manuscripts on Papyrus of the Greek Bible,* ed. Frederic G. Kenyon. Fasciculus 3 supplement, Pauline Epistles (London: Walker, 1936/37).

14. A good survey of the most important observations and arguments is provided by Werner Georg Kümmel, *Introduction to the New Testament* rev. ed. (Nashville: Abingdon, 1975), §24.3.

15. The translation is quoted from *The Epistles of St. Clement of Rome and St. Ignatius of Antioch,* ed. James A. Kleist (Ancient Christian Writers, 1; Westminster, Md: Newman, 1946), p. 95. PolPhil 4,3 provides a passage where Polycarp, the bishop of Smyrna at the time Ignatius writes to Smyrna, describes the duties of a "widow." This provides a proof beyond doubt that widows represented a special ministry in Smyrna at the beginning of the second century C.E.

16. *The Geneva Bible: The Annotated New Testament, 1602 Edition,* ed. Gerald T. Sheppard; reprint of a 1607 printing of the third edition of 1602 (New York: Pilgrim Press, 1989).

17. Eusebius, *H.E.* 6:14:2.

18. The translation is taken from *A New Eusebius: Documents Illustrative*

of the History of the Church to A.D. 337, ed. J. Stevenson (London: SPCK, 1980⁹), 223.

19. Klaus Berger, "Apostelbrief und apostolische Rede: Zum Formular frühchristlicher Briefe," *ZNW* 65 (1974), 190–231.

20. Jeffrey H. Loria, *What's It All About, Charlie Brown? Peanuts Kids Look at America Today* (Greenwich, Conn.: Fawcett Publications, 1968).

21. Based on *The Greek New Testament,* ed. K. Aland, M. Black, C. M. Martini, B. M. Metzger, A. Wikgren. 2d ed. (Stuttgart: Württemberg Bibelanstalt, 1968) as provided on computer disk by *Facility for Computer Analysis of Texts* at the University of Pennsylvania, Philadelphia, Version 0.1 (4/24/86 rak). The spaces are not counted to simulate the *scriptio continua* of the oldest manuscripts, but the *nomina sacra* are not abbreviated.

22. This analysis unexpectedly provides support to the theory of Edgar J. Goodspeed. Goodspeed proposed an old collection of the letters of Paul that began with the letter to the Ephesians. His argument is based on the introductory character of Ephesians: "Out of 618 short phrases into which Ephesians may be conveniently broken for detailed comparison with the Pauline letters, 550 have unmistakable parallels in Paul, in words or substance" (*The Meaning of Ephesians,* 9). "It seems abundantly clear that the epistle is full of matters . . . which blossom into full significance if the epistle be understood as an introduction to the Pauline letters, when first they were offered to the churches" (*The Meaning of Ephesians,* 73). The most difficult part of this theory, which was widely accepted by English speaking scholars but had almost no influence on German exegetes, is that there is no manuscript evidence to prove the existence of an edition with nine letters (lacking Hebrews and the Pastoral letters) that started out with the letter to the Ephesians. However, if my analysis is correct the letter to the Ephesians functions as an introduction to the expanded edition of thirteen letters because it is the first letter of the appendix. See J. E. Goodspeed, *The Meaning of Ephesians* (Chicago: University of Chicago Press, 1933); "The Editio Princeps of Paul," *JBL* 64 (1945), 193–204; "Ephesians and the First Edition of Paul," *JBL* 70 (1951), 285–91; *A History of Early Christian Literature,* revised and enlarged by Robert M. Grant (Chicago: University of Chicago Press, 1966); *The Formation of the New Testament* (Chicago: University of Chicago Press, 1926), 2d ed. 1927; *An Introduction to the New Testament* (Chicago: University of Chicago Press, 1937), 15th ed. 1966. See also John Knox, *Philemon Among the Letters of Paul: A New View of Its Place and Importance* (Chicago: University of Chicago Press, 1935). A summary of Goodspeed's theory in relation to older theories is provided by C. L. Mitton, *The Formation of the Pauline Corpus of Letters* (London: Epworth Press, 1955). The most inclusive survey of modern exegetical works on the formation of the corpus Paulinum I know of is presented by E. H. Lovering, *The Collection, Redaction, and Early Circulation of the Corpus Paulinum* (Ann Arbor: UMI Southern Methodist University, 1988).

23. The Latin text of the passage reads: *Mearum epistularum nulla est συναγωγή; sed habet Tiro instar septuaginta; et quidem sunt a te quaedam sumendae. eas ego oportet perspiciam, corrigam; tum denique edidentur.* Taken from Marcus Tullius Cicero, *Atticus-Briefe,* ed. Helmut Kasten, 3d ed. (München: Heimeran, 1980), 1052.

24. The data is taken from Karl Büchner, "M. Tullius Cicero: Briefe," *PRE* 2.13 (1939), 1192–1235.

25. Nepos died after 27 B.C. He describes his visit in *Atticus* 25:16.

26. Karl Büchner, "M. Tullius Cicero: Briefe," *PRE* 2.13 (1939), 1224–25.

27. The editorial changes taking place during the preparation of a second edition demonstrate typical editorial activity of authors like nothing else. Here it is possible to study tendencies authors of letter collections must have felt as well. The only book I know of that carried the evidence together is Hilarius Emonds, *Zweite Auflage im Altertum: Kulturgeschichtliche Studien zur Überlieferung der antiken Literatur* (Leipzig: Harrasowitz, 1941). The example of Jerome and Rufinus is taken from this book (p.48).

28. An elaborate analysis of the philological argument is given by Niels Hyldahl, "Die Frage nach der literarischen Einheit des 2. Korintherbriefes," *ZNW* 64 (1973), 289–306.

29. An excellent study of the final wishes and the end of the letter to the Romans is presented by Harry Gamble Jr., *The Textual History of the Letter to the Romans: A Study in Textual and Literary Criticism* (StD 42; Grand Rapids: Eerdmans, 1977).

30. A list of Greek letters is given by Chan-Hie Kim, "Index of Greek Papyrus Letters," *Studies in Ancient Letter Writing, Semeia* 22 (1982), 102–12. A survey of results from recent research and a comprehensive bibliography are presented by Klaus Berger, "Hellenistische Gattungen im Neuen Testament," *Aufstieg und Niedergang der römischen Welt* 25.2 (Berlin, New York: De Gruyter, 1984), 1326–40. Important studies on formal criteria concerning letters are P. Schubert, *Form and Function of the Pauline Thanksgivings* (BZNW 20; Berlin: Töpelmann, 1939); G. A. Eschlimann, "La rédaction des épîtres pauliniennes," *RB* 53 (1946), 185–96; J. T. Sanders, "The Transition from Opening Epistolary Thanksgiving to Body in the Letters of the Pauline Corpus," *JBL* 81 (1962), 348–62; T. Y. Mullins, "Disclosure: A Literary Form in the New Testament," *NT* 7 (1964/65), 44–50; G. J. Bahr, "Paul and Letter Writing in the Fifth (sic! correct: First) Century," *CBQ* 18 (1966), 465–77; R. W. Funk, "The Apostolic *Parousia*: Form and Significance," *Christian History and Interpretation: Studies presented to John Knox,* ed. W. R. Farmer, C. F. D. Moule, R. R. Niebuhr (Cambridge: University Press, 1967), 249–68; G. J. Bahr, "The Subscriptions in the Pauline Letters," *JBL* 87 (1968), 27–41; Carl J. Bjerkelund, *Parakalô: Form, Funktion und Sinn der parakalô-Sätze in den paulinischen Briefen* (BTN 1; Oslo, Bergen, Tromsö: Universitätsverlag, 1967); J. L. White, "Introductory Formulae in the Body of the Pauline Letter," *JBL* 90 (1971), 91–97; J. L. White, K. A. Kensinger, "Categories of Greek Papyrus

Letters." *SBL 1976 Seminar Papers*, 10, ed. George MacRae (Missoula: Scholars Press, 1976), 79–91.

31. Further examples from the Letters of Ignatius: *IgnRom* 8:3 and 10:3. In these cases Ignatius refers to the letter he is just finishing.

32. Usually 2 Cor 7:5 is regarded as a new beginning. This view is almost always dependent on the argument that 2 Cor 7:5 picks up where 2 Cor 2:12-13 left off and therefore is part of the same letter as 2:12-13. 2 Cor 2:14—7:4 is regarded as a digression. If one looks at 7:4 without these presuppositions, it is evident that no conjunction relates 7:4 to the preceding text, whereas no fewer than four expressions of 7:4 are picked up in the following sentences: καύχησις in 7:14; παράκλησις in 7:6.7.13; χαρά in 7:7.9.13.16; θλίψις in 7:5. 7:5 is excellently connected to 7:4 with καὶ γὰρ as far as syntax and contents is concerned. Paul's change of attitude towards the Corinthians takes place between 7:2-3 and 7:4.

33. Hans Dieter Betz, *Galatians: A Commentary on Paul's Letter to the Churches in Galatia* (Philadelphia: Fortress, 1979).

34. NIV gives "men" instead of "people."

35. For a detailed investigation into sociological aspects of early Christian missionaries, see Gerd Theissen, "Legitimation and Subsistence: An Essay on the Sociology of Early Christian Missionaries," *The Social Setting of Pauline Christianity: Essays on Corinth* (Philadelphia: Fortress, 1982), 27-67.

36. Paul devotes an entire chapter of his authorized recension of 1 Corinthians (Chapter 9) to defend his way of financing his ministry. This chapter forms one of those passages that I call unexpected digressions. If we delete it the surrounding text reads more smoothly. The topic of Paul's way of financing his mission is only loosely related to the context. Like 1 Corinthians 13, I understand this chapter as a passage that Paul added when he prepared his authorized recension of the Corinthian correspondence for friends in Ephesus.

37. Most of this fictive letter consists of quotes from the letters of Paul that have been treated in this book.

Index

Ancient Sources

Ancient Manuscripts and Old Editions